TASTE & TECHNIQUE IN
BOOK-COLLECTING

The Sandars Lectures in Bibliography
1947

TASTE & TECHNIQUE IN BOOK-COLLECTING

A study of recent developments in Great Britain and the United States

BY

JOHN CARTER

SANDARS READER IN BIBLIOGRAPHY
AND SOMETIME SCHOLAR OF
KING'S COLLEGE

CAMBRIDGE
AT THE UNIVERSITY PRESS
1949

PUBLISHED BY
THE SYNDICS OF THE CAMBRIDGE UNIVERSITY PRESS
London Office: Bentley House, N.W.1
Published in U.S.A. by the R. R. Bowker Co.

Agents for Canada, India, and Pakistan: Macmillan

First edition   1948
Second impression, corrected 1949

Printed in Great Britain at the University Press, Cambridge
(Brooke Crutchley, University Printer)

To My Wife

CONTENTS

CONTENTS.

vii.

PREFACE

Τίς τίνι ταῦτα λέγεις; says Paulus Silentiarius in one of the epigrams in the Palatine Anthology: who are you and to whom are you speaking? A critic has a duty [1] to present his credentials, as well as to define his terms of reference, before presuming on his readers' attention; and I shall do both as briefly as I can.

Except for the duration of the war, I have for the past twenty years earned my living in the rare book business, as European buying agent for an American firm. I was a book-collector for five years before that and have maintained one or two specialities since. I have also published some contributions to bibliographical and bibliophilic literature, as by-products of my work. But the following pages represent the reflexions not of a book-collector or a bibliographer or a man of letters, but of a professional dealer. Some readers may think that there is too much here about sales and the state of the market: but book-collecting means book-buying. Others may consider that I have over-estimated the influence of the bookseller in collecting history: but it is commonly under-estimated and it can in some important respects hardly be de Ricci, who was a bibliographer first and a dealer second, I am the first member of the rare book trade to have been appointed Sandars Reader; and whatever my diffidence as the representative of a business in which I recognise my betters, it is one to which I should be happy to do some credit.

My second obligation to my readers is to make quite clear what this book does and what it does not attempt to do. It is not a history of book-collecting. That has still to be written. I have quoted here and there from the historians and commentators, and my survey of the past century is naturally cast in a roughly historical form. But many, and many important, names and collections and happenings find no place here because they seemed to me to have less bearing

[1] Cf. Cyril Connolly, *Enemies of Promise* (1938).

than others superficially less important on those developments of taste and technique which can be seen in retrospect to have influenced book-collecting as we know it today.

Furthermore, this study of the evolution and present state of book-collecting is restricted to Great Britain and the United States. I know that Continental collectors, bibliographers and booksellers have influenced the course of bibliophilic history, especially in the fields of early printing and illustration, of bindings and (more recently) of scientific and technical literature. But I am not competent to assess that influence; and fortunately it is primarily in the fields of their own literature and thought that the most significant recent developments in English and American collecting have lain. Early printed books were being collected in England before Dibdin was born: post-Elizabethan first editions were only just beginning to be collected when he died. I know also that a few English and American collectors have followed the French tradition, which has therefore had some influence in both countries. But its influence has been strictly limited, not only by the small number of its adherents but even more by its own rigid insularity both of taste and technique.

Finally, and perhaps most important, this is not a primer or a text-book or a manual for beginners, nor is it a piece of propaganda for book-collecting. There have been plenty of primers in the last fifty years, so that the novice is well cared for. And if my patron, Samuel Sandars, ever considered that book-collecting needed any propaganda, he surely would not have regarded his Readership as exaggerated. Moreover, with the partial exception of Seymour a suitable platform for it. But I believe that the essential nature of book-collecting, the play of cause and effect in its development, the evolution and also the rationale of our present technical approach to it, could all do with more thought than they sometimes receive. This book therefore, which is an attempt to analyse some of these aspects of book-collecting, inevitably takes a good deal for granted. I have not cluttered up my pages or slowed down my argument to explain the meaning of *incunabula* or cancels, of Strawberry Hill or *STC*, and anyone to whom such terms need explanation should be warned now that he has the wrong book. Yet the fact that I have aimed at a thoughtful and a moderately knowledgeable audience does not mean that I consider myself an expert, for I do not. Nor does it mean that I do not cherish hopes that a somewhat ruminative treatise on book-collecting may be found of some interest to others besides addicts, for I do.

My third obligation, always a pleasant one, is to acknowledge my various debts. Something of what I owe to other writers is indicated by quotations in the text or by references to their works in the notes. But for assistance which is inevitably invisible to the reader I have to thank Mr F. S. Ferguson and Professor William A. Jackson, who scrutinised Chapters I–V; Mr Michael Sadleir, with whom Chapter XI was extensively discussed; and Messrs John Hayward, John Sparrow and Dudley Massey, from whose comments on the first draft the whole book has benefited greatly. I have also profited from the views of Mr Percy Muir, Mr A. N. L. Munby and Mr E. P. Goldschmidt on the final draft; Mr Goldschmidt's being all the more valuable to me for his amiable but profound disapproval of my whole treatment of my subject.

It is rightly considered superfluous to thank the Cambridge University Press for being either affable or efficient; but I shall nevertheless permit myself the pleasure of doing so.

In conclusion, two technical details require notice. The place of publication of any book referred to may be assumed to be London unless otherwise indicated. In citing collected books as examples of this and that, I am normally speaking of the original edition, and exceptions (e.g. the Jenson *Pliny* or the 1532 *Chaucer*) will be sufficiently obvious.

JOHN CARTER

DEFINITION OF
A BOOK-COLLECTOR

Take care not to understand editions and title-pages too well.
LORD CHESTERFIELD

Bibliophiles, an idiotic class. A. E. HOUSMAN

A. W. POLLARD once [1] defined book-collecting as 'the bringing together of books which in their contents, their form or the history of the individual copy possess some element of permanent interest, and either actually or prospectively are rare, in the sense of being difficult to procure. This qualification of rarity [he continued], which figures much too largely in the popular view of book-collecting, is entirely subordinate to that of interest, for the rarity of a book devoid of interest is a matter of no concern. On the other hand, so long as a book (or anything else) is and appears likely to continue to be easily procurable at any moment, no one has any reason for collecting it. The anticipation that it will always be easily procurable is often unfounded; but so long as the anticipation exists it restrains collecting, with the result that Horn-books are much rarer than First Folio Shakespeares.'

In the course of the same admirable article (at once, *more suo*, learned and humane) Pollard noted that while by the end of the seventeenth century book-collecting was in full swing all over Europe and much of its elementary apparatus already in existence —book-auctions, for instance, were introduced to England from Holland before 1680—it was 'rather as an added grace in the formation of a fine library than as a separate pursuit'. And it is precisely the isolation of the special quality which distinguishes book-collecting from discrimination or good taste exercised in the formation of a library, that I have looked for in vain among the histories and handbooks. Enthusiasts and critics, *illuminati* and

[1] *Encyclopaedia Britannica*, 11th ed., s.v. 'Book-Collecting'.

philistines alike habitually speak and write about book-collecting as if its essential nature were perfectly well understood and its practitioners as clearly definable as pharmaceutical chemists or officers of the Royal Navy. This is not so. Yet if we are to consider book-collecting practically as well as historically, we must surely give some thought to what we mean by the term. We must decide which mere accumulators of books we shall exclude altogether, which library-formers qualify and which do not, which specialists we shall relegate to the annex; where, in short, we shall draw the line.

In some, bibliophily is induced by circumstances, for others it is contagious, in others again it is a natural by-product or development from the process of forming a library. No one, I think, would contend that book-collectors are born rather than made. Hereditary bibliophily is of the rarest occurrence in history,[1] and the exceptions are so pitifully few that even Lysenko would have to label them as sports rather than as instances of the inheritance of acquired characteristics. On the other hand, a collector cannot be made, whether by his own or another's effort, out of unsuitable material, any more than silk purses can be made out of sows' ears. There is undoubtedly a greater tendency for book-collecting to take root and flourish in persons of studious or reflective temper than among pugilists or aviators; and certain professions, like surgery and the law, seem especially favourable to it. But even were there not in fact numerous examples of its luxuriant growth among men of action and of affairs—Lord Rosebery and Lord Keynes, J. P. Morgan and Henry E. Huntington, Mazarin and Louis Barthou—this is rather a question of soil and cultivation than of the seed itself. And if we are trying to define the book-collector, we must look first for his motive source.

Mr Harold Nicolson recently[2] maintained that there is no such thing as the 'collector's instinct', a phrase worn threadbare in extenuation of many aimless as well as many purposeful accumulative activities; and although he was writing as an admittedly

---

[1] This is perhaps less absolutely true in France than in England or America, and even in England we must not forget the Thorolds and the Earls of Crawford.

[2] *Spectator*, 7 February 1947. Mr Nicolson has since, I am glad to say, suffered a partial conversion.

hostile witness, blind to the charm of original boards and openly contemptuous of philately, he was in this contention surely perfectly correct. Magpies have an acquisitive instinct, and a similarly indiscriminate passion for accumulating junk afflicts one in a hundred of the human race. But that is not what we mean by a collector. The competitive spirit, which is a normal and unexceptionable characteristic of the book-collector *vis-à-vis* other book-collectors, is certainly a very common, if not a universal, human instinct; and I am inclined to think that this factor, by an illegitimate extension of the ingredient to the whole, may account for the prevalence of a phrase which not only has an apologetic sound—as who should say 'he was cross-eyed from birth, poor fellow'—but also promotes an erroneous conception of the nature of the book-collector.

Mr Nicolson makes another point which bears, though less directly, on our quest for a definition. He maintains that bibliophiles suffer from the consciousness of being a minority, even a persecuted minority, and that this causes them to adopt, in respect of their propensity, a generally defensive attitude toward the rest of the world. Again, and regretfully, I think he is right. Moreover, I suspect that to the intrinsic difficulty of defining a particularly elusive sentiment or motive has often been added a disinclination to expose any such definition to public scrutiny, for fear of public ridicule. For many a true bibliophile regards bibliophily as in some sense a mystery,[1] not only too complicated but also too delicate, almost too sacred, to make its exposition to the uninitiated anything but painful. It is in the same spirit that he sometimes hesitates to show his books to strangers, and this by no means entirely (as is often supposed) because he is sure they will drop them or spill whisky over them. It is always instructive to watch a collector's face when he has handed some treasure to a visitor: one who has expressed interest, who may even have come well recommended, but who is not certainly known to be initiate. For a man's handling of a book is as instantly revealing to the experienced eye as his grasp on the reins of a horse.

[1] See, for instance, Richard Curle, *Collecting American First Editions* (1930), p. 212, and John Drinkwater, in his preface to vol. IV of the *Ashley Catalogue*.

This diffidence, this tendency to distrust, in the matter of book-collecting, anyone not himself a collector, and the resultant cliquishness—these are all regrettable. They are also, I submit, irrational and unnecessary. Society is composed of minorities, so that book-collectors have plenty of company in that respect: and though gardeners may tend, like any other technicians, to talk shop very happily when they find themselves in company with others of their kind, I doubt whether they have been accused (as Mr Nicolson accused book-collectors) of emitting a distinctive note or of showing signs of minority-consciousness. Book-collecting can, and occasionally does, degenerate into biblio-mania,[1] which, like any other mania, makes for better stories than the doings of sane men. Such quirks may sometimes need explanation: but to regard them as needing excuse is to admit, mistakenly, that they are normal. We have been dogged since Lucian's time by certain general misconceptions, such as that bibliophiles never read their books,[2] but acquire them out of intellectual snobbery or for the pleasure of inspiring a fellow-bibliophile with envy; and by certain particular misconceptions, like the confusion between the terms 'uncut' and 'unopened', which seem to support the accusation of illiteracy. Indeed, the justification for accumulating in the Folger Library about eighty copies of the *First Folio*, or in the Library of the University of Illinois more than fifty first editions of *Paradise Lost*, is not immediately apparent to the layman and may need some exposition even to a collector. Yet here what seems to be senseless greed—and Folger certainly had a streak of the miser in him—can be shown to have a scholarly value. And in general, if the debt which literature and history owe to bibliography is now generally recognised, as it is, so also is the debt which all three owe to book-collecting.

Many scholars have borne witness to this debt. I shall cite only two examples. 'It is by the zeal of collectors', says A. W. Pollard,[3]

[1] About which Holbrook Jackson has written a book as rich in plums (and as indigestible in large helpings) as a Christmas pudding: *The Anatomy of Biblio-mania* (1930, revised edition 1932).

[2] 'When Locker-Lampson complained to Bedford that a book which he had bound for him did not shut properly, Bedford exclaimed, *Why bless me, sir, you've been reading it!*' Jackson, op. cit. (1932 ed.), p. 719.   [3] Loc. cit.

'that books which otherwise would have perished from neglect are discovered, cared for and preserved, and those who achieve these results certainly deserve well of the community.' And Professor F. A. Pottle, in the preface to the work[1] in which he classically demonstrated the dependence of biography upon the bibliographer, has this to say of those on whom bibliographers in their turn depend: 'I have the greatest respect for [dealers and collectors], and I consider that the scholar of today who makes remarks about "mere collectors" is talking nonsense. Our science of bibliography would be sadly hampered, indeed, were it not for the generous and largely disinterested service which private collectors perform by buying and putting freely at our disposal books which our public libraries cannot or will not purchase.' In return, the attitude of the collector towards scholarship could hardly be more delightfully expressed than in the note[2] which Thomas Hollis, a great book-collector and a great patron of learning, wrote in a book he was presenting to Harvard: 'A fine copy of a rare work. It cost a guinea. T.H. is fond of sending Lexicons and Grammars to Harvard College, in honor of those *first-rate* Scholars, possibly half a dozen, the noblest of all men, who, he trusts, are now forming there.' Conscious of beneficence, proud of the quality of his gift, Hollis's 'fondness' was based on a trust in scholarship which events have abundantly justified.

From the days when George Thomason collected and preserved, as they came out, every ephemeral pamphlet and tract of the Civil War period in England to the bequest to Princeton of the Parrish collection of Victorian fiction, the gift of Arthur William Young's library to Cambridge, or the depositing in the British Museum of the late Mr Barry Ono's collection of 'penny dreadfuls', the history of book-collecting is a record of service by book-collectors —a service performed sometimes deliberately, sometimes unconsciously—to the republic of letters. The book-collector is in fact one of the assault troops in literature's and history's battle against the inequity of oblivion. 'The pulping-mill', wrote W. Carew Hazlitt,[3]

[1] *The Literary Career of James Boswell* (Oxford, 1929), p. xvii.
[2] *Harvard Library Bulletin*, vol. i, no. i (Cambridge, Mass., 1947), p. 53.
[3] *The Book-Collector* (1904), p. 18.

'has been as busy as the Press all these centuries on which we look back. It has neither eyes nor ears, nor has it compassion; it unrelentingly grinds and consumes all that comes in its way; age after age it has reduced to dust what the men of the time refuse in the presence of something newer, and, as they hold, better.' From Archbishop Parker and Robert Cotton to our own time, collectors, whether the professionals in the institutional libraries or the amateurs who are our present concern, have been preservers of books and essential contributors to the progress of scholarship.

Their technique has been well described by a now old-fashioned but still respectable authority, John Hill Burton.[1] 'It is', he says, 'the general ambition of the class to find value where there seems to be none, and this develops a certain skill and subtlety, enabling the operator, in the midst of a heap of rubbish, to put his finger on those things which have in them the latent capacity to become valuable and curious. The adept will at once intuitively separate from its friends the book that either is or will become curious. And there must be something more than mere rarity to give it this value.' Note the words 'or will become curious'; for it was then and is still one of the collector's most significant functions to anticipate the scholar and the historian, to find some interest where none was recognised before, to rescue books from obscurity, to pioneer a subject or an author by seeking out and assembling the raw material for study, in whatever its printed form. It is a very easy matter nowadays to find a First Folio or a first edition of Johnson's Dictionary and a man needs neither imagination nor persistence to possess himself of a copy of either: all he needs is a cheque-book. Similarly it was very easy to stand an egg on end after Columbus showed how it was done. But as Mr Sadleir[2] put it, rather more pithily than Burton: 'In nature the bird who gets up earliest catches the most worms, but in book-collecting the prizes fall to birds who know worms when they see them.'

[1] The Book-Hunter (1862), p. 209.
[2] Michael Sadleir, 'Decentralisation or Deadlock', in The Colophon, no. 3 (New York, 1930).

Yet all these factors and qualities are equally applicable to a good institutional librarian with money behind him or to any man who brings 'an added grace to the formation of a fine library'. In search of what Pollard called the 'separate pursuit' of book-collecting, we must go deeper. For while it is true that an original edition in original state can tell the bibliographer, and perhaps through him the historian or critic, something about the book and its author which could not be learned from a rebound copy or a later edition, the fact remains that a poor copy, which he can bend in half or even pull apart if he needs to, will serve his purpose at least as well as, and probably better than, a fine one. But it is the latter and not the former that the collector desires. If he is a collector of fine printing, or of fine bindings, or of illustrated books, his insistence on the highest attainable quality in the objects of his pursuit hardly needs explanation, let alone extenuation. But the first editions of *King Lear* or *The Pilgrim's Progress*, of *The Dunciad* or *Wuthering Heights*, are conspicuously lacking in physical appeal to the uninitiated eye; and it is crucial to our quest for the definition of the book-collector *pur sang* to consider why (*a*) he so passionately wants one of those books in its original edition at all, and (*b*) why he attaches so much importance to its being bibliographically correct in all material points of edition and issue and in as nearly as possible the same physical condition as on the day it first appeared.

As a starting-point for this further narrowing down we may quote Pollard once more. 'To attract a collector,' he says, 'a book must appeal to his eye, his mind, or his imagination.' The appeal to the eye is, as we have already remarked, a motive which the layman can more readily understand, for in this respect the appreciation of books does not differ in kind, though it may in degree, from the appreciation of pictures or silver or porcelain. It is the way in which the collector's mind (or studious interests) and imagination (or heart) are engaged, and the means by which these express themselves, that bring us to grips with our problem. For it does not matter whether your affection is for the moment centred on Bacon's *Essays* or *Sherlock Holmes* or *Das Kapital*: you will express your affection, if you are a book-collector, by acquiring the original edition, however many later editions you may need or possess for purposes of study. Similarly, if your interest is for the moment centred on the development of chancery italic types in the sixteenth century or on the economics of cheap fiction series in the nineteenth, its logical expression, if you are a collector as distinct from a researcher, is to seek out and possess yourself of every pertinent example you can hear of and lay hands on. As Dr Chapman has well put it:[1] 'It is admitted that literature and history cannot be adequately studied in modern books alone. Even if modern editions were adequate in the information they furnish—and notoriously they are not—they do not satisfy that Sense of the Past without which the study of literature and history is unimaginative and formal. That the student should have some access to originals is necessary for practical purposes, and necessary also for his spiritual health.'

The imagination and the mind cannot always be precisely separated, in book-collecting or elsewhere. But for simplicity's sake we will consider them as potentially distinct components of our equation, as is, more obviously, the eye. There is, however, an important further component to be added, and that is connoisseurship. For whereas the other three may be combined or may obtain in pairs or separately, some degree of connoisseurship or expertise is always present; it is in fact what the mathematicians call, I believe, a constant in the equation.

Some may think the word connoisseurship has a snobbish sound, and I would use a four-letter Saxon equivalent if such existed. All it means is the ability to distinguish good from bad, the significant from the commonplace, in the same kind, with some concomitant satisfaction in the exercise of that ability. An engineer who can tell a sound casting from a flawed one, a soldier who can tell a sniper from a tree-stump, a housewife who can tell under-cut from scrag-end, are all connoisseurs in that they apply some degree of skill, born of precept and observation, to a given problem in their own field. In a precisely similar sense, and with no more affectation whatsoever, does a man distinguish—with a preference for the best and experience as his guide—a vintage port from a non-

[1] R. W. Chapman, 'The Sense of the Past', in *The Book-Collector's Quarterly*, no. 3 (1930), p. 51.

vintage, a Rembrandt from a Bol or a pristine copy of *Pride and Prejudice* in the original boards from a rebound copy without the half-titles.

Whether the heart, the mind or the eye be the predominant factor in any individual collector's make-up; whether connoisseurship, or the application of technique, plays a large or a lesser part in his approach to his objective; there have been few bibliophiles who will not be found to conform to this general formula. For 'books are more than reading matter,' as A. J. A. Symons [1] observed, 'just as clothes are more than coverings. And just as clothes can have, over and above their purpose of covering, the two attributes of style and durability (cut and texture), so books may add either beauty of form, or what we may call interest of edition, to the text they hold.' The analogy between bibliophily and dandyism might well be explored further, for there is a distinct conformity between the plain calf or plain boards beloved of the fastidious collector and Sir Max Beerbohm's famous analysis of Brummell's supreme elegance—'certain congruities of dark cloth and a rigid perfection of linen'.

The book-collector, then, is not just an eccentric who prefers one edition to another for some ritually compulsive reason. He is not a man who says simply 'the old is better' or who thinks that rarity is an objective in itself. It is not even enough to say that he is a man who is not as well satisfied with a photographic reproduction of the original, or a roll of microfilm, or a well-edited verbatim reprint, as with the genuine article. He is rather a man (or of course a woman, though bibliophily, like dandyism, is less common among women) who has a reverence for, and a desire to possess, the original or some other specifically admirable, curious or interesting edition of a book he loves or respects or one which has a special place among his intellectual interests. And the book must be either in its original state or in some contemporary, associative or otherwise appropriate condition. Furthermore, he

[1] 'A Book-Collector's Apology', in *The Book-Collector's Quarterly*, no. 1 (1930), p. 51.

enjoys, with a degree of intensity which will vary according to his temperament, his training and the standards of his fellow-bibliophiles, that exercise of his natural and intellectual faculties which is involved in the application of knowledge, observation, ingenuity, foresight, enterprise and persistence to the pursuit of his quarry, its scrutiny and appraisal when found, its use and perhaps formal description when secured. But above all and pervading all is the element recognised in the second half of the very word bibliophile. Indeed, the Greeks might almost have been justified in invoking ἔρως to describe the feeling which animates the true book-collector: that kind of love which demands the physical possession of its object, which consumes the collector with passionate longings, chills him with fear of his rivals, tortures him with envy. Bibliophily is on the whole a civilised pursuit, yet its votaries know the heights and the depths.

The objects of book-collectors' attention have always been of an infinite variety. Their own attitude, and that of the public, towards their collections has changed with changing tastes and conventions. The degree and direction of the connoisseurship applied to book-collecting—that is, method and skill as distinct from motive—have developed and will continue to develop. These evolutions of taste and technique during the past century are the subject of the following chapters. But the love of books for their own sake is much more than a mere hundred years old; and whether or not we are any nearer to defining a book-collector, we must recognise that certain emotions, aspirations and principles are fundamental to his nature and persist through the changing taste and practice of each succeeding generation.

PART I: EVOLUTION

CHAPTER I

ROXBURGHE TO ROWFANT

Dread, my dear Lady Louisa, that in preferring some comely quarto to a shabby duodecimo your ladyship may be rejecting the 'editio princeps'.
SIR WALTER SCOTT

O N 18 November 1847, just over a century ago, died the Reverend Thomas Frognall Dibdin, the most enthusiastic and the most prolific chronicler, anecdotist and publicist in the history of bibliophily. He had, indeed, outlived the heyday of that type of book-collecting which he lovingly celebrated in a series of ample and splendidly printed, though bibliographically not always reliable, volumes: yet his passing serves to mark the end of a golden age and the beginning of what we may call the pre-history of book-collecting as we know it today.

Despite some notable exceptions,[1] collectors in England until late in the eighteenth century had generally tended to think in terms of eventual public ownership of their books. Libraries formed on the grand scale would be bequeathed to the nation, like Sir Hans Sloane's 50,000 volumes or the magnificent collection of early printed books, upwards of 20,000 in number, which the British Museum received as late as 1846 from Thomas Grenville, who, dying at ninety-one, was perhaps the last of his kind. But even the special collections of less wealthy men were apt to follow this public-spirited fashion: Garrick's plays went to the British Museum, Malone's Shakesperian collection was left to the Bodleian and Capell's to Trinity College, Cambridge.

The glittering circle hymned (it is the only word) by Dibdin— whether aristocrats like the Marquess of Blandford[2] or commoners

[1] E.g. Harley, Narcissus Luttrell, Dr Richard Mead.

[2] I shall not burden the text with initials, dates or other details of most of the collectors mentioned in this and the following chapters, all of which, and much more, may be found in Seymour de Ricci's *English Collectors of Books and Manuscripts, 1530–1930* (Cambridge, 1930). This is an essential reference book, based on the Sandars Lectures for 1929–30, to which my indebtedness in this chapter will be as obvious as it was inevitable.

like William Beckford—while quite rich enough to afford such public beneficence, were less disposed to it. It is clear that a new conception was abroad in the second and third quarters of the century; that of the personal collection, which would either be kept in the family, as were Thorold's and Miller's and Holford's, or dispersed after the collector's own use and enjoyment of it, as were Richard Heber's and most of Halliwell's. 'Broadly speaking,' says Hazlitt,[1] 'we recognise two varieties of collector from all time: the one who confers his name on a library, and the other whose library confers a name on him.' As we look back on the past century, the majority of collectors certainly seem to fall into the latter category (a not ignoble one); but we cannot doubt that the original members of the Roxburghe Club and many of their successors aspired to the former.

The celebrated Roxburghe sale occupied 42 consecutive weekdays from May to early July of the year 1812. It was a battle of Homeric quality and Dibdin was its rhapsodist. The 9353 lots brought £23,397. 10s. 6d.; and the Valdarfer *Boccaccio* fetched £2260, an auction record for a printed book which stood for seventy-two years. The record itself is not important. But the book which made it is significant, since it typifies the taste of a generation. For observe: the Roxburghe copy of the *First Folio* of Shakespeare brought £100, and that was high for the period;[2] while the First Quartos of *Much Ado about Nothing*, *The Merchant of Venice* and *Richard II*, made £2. 17s., £10 and £7. 7s. respectively. If the Roxburghe sale was the first great sale of modern times, it was also the last manifesto of a closing era of taste, in which the effective criteria of the great collectors were not so much literary as physical. They paid a good deal of attention, certainly, to *editiones principes* of the classics and to the rare early romances: but the main objectives of the majority were the splendours of early printing and illumination, fine bindings by the great masters, early illustration, vellum copies, Aldines and tall Elzevirs and the like.

[1] Op. cit., p. 88.
[2] Hazlitt wrote in 1904 (op. cit., p. 302): 'Even in our time and memory, the first folio could be had in fine state for £50 or £60.'

Richard Heber was a man of very different stamp: an omnivorous reader, a great scholar, a passionate collector. If his predecessors and contemporaries were distinguished, often scholarly, and generally judicious amateurs (in the French sense), Heber was much more. For he collected literature and history, English and foreign, in first and other rare editions, with the utmost catholicity of scope, if with a somewhat less scrupulous connoisseurship. His ideal was to own three copies of every book, one for the cabinet, one for use and one to lend to his friends. And he died with four houses full of books in England as well as several more on the Continent. Yet his influence, or the development of taste which he foreshadowed, had made so little headway that the sale of his library (1834-7) was a financial failure. We must not, of course, overlook the fact that the high prices of the Roxburghe sale period reflect the generally inflationary economic conditions of the Napoleonic wars, which gave place to the deflation so graphically described in Dibdin's *Bibliophobia* (1832). Indeed, the general economic state of the country has always governed the rise and fall of book-prices like those of any other commodity, so that the disappointing results achieved by (for instance) the Ashburnham sales in 1898 or the Adams sale in 1931 were due as much to the financial slumps of 1897 and 1930 as to any temperamental apathy of taste among buyers. When Heber's books were sold, the 'cometary period' (as Hazlitt called it), the glamorous boom of the first quarter of the century, was over; and the collectors of the next generation who were so powerfully to influence mid-century bibliophily—men like Corser, Dyce and Daniel, Utterson, Halliwell and Tite—were either not yet in action or provided insufficient competition for so tremendous a dispersal.

One man, however, saw his opportunity and seized it with both hands. W. H. Miller—'Measure Miller', as he was called, from the pocket foot-rule which always accompanied him—was easily the biggest buyer at the sixteen sales of the Heber library, and from the wreckage of that vast and rambling edifice were laid the foundations of what was later known as the Britwell Library, the greatest collection of the century of rare early English books. Miller's active period occupied only about twenty-five years. And though more recent collectors, like Huntington, may (with the help of bulk purchases) [1] have collected faster, hardly Sir Thomas Phillipps himself, who once bought 16,000 manuscripts in one year, can in his own century have rivalled him for intensity.

These repeated references to auction sales must not be taken to imply that the collecting world did not continue during these years to depend, as it always will, mainly on the antiquarian booksellers. It is rather that an important sale, in addition to offering a well-publicised opportunity to collectors at the time, is a useful signpost to the historian. If he is looking forward, the new collectors can be measured in the activity of their agents; if backward, it is by studying its catalogue that he can acquire, as a faint substitute for that vivid impression only offered by the sight of the books themselves, some idea of the taste and methods of the man who formed the collection. Yet at all times collectors' technique certainly, and taste often, has been influenced by the booksellers with whom they deal. Beckford's letters to George Clarke [2] disclose, it is true, an autocrat, as confident of his own connoisseurship as he was sometimes perverse in its direction, giving orders to a tradesman. But Beckford, as poor Clarke must have been thankful sometimes to remember, was an exception to most rules; and the function of Lilly, Longman or Toovey, of Bohn, Thorp or Payne and Foss was by no means restricted to issuing catalogues, executing commissions, offering books by post and keeping open shop.

Indeed, a bookseller's catalogue reflects a double aspect of contemporary taste: his own, which, if he is a good bookseller, will be influential; and also his customers', which, if he is a shrewd one, will be faithfully catered for. And it may therefore be instructive to survey briefly, as an example, the catalogue of one very enterprising bookseller, William Pickering, issued (neatly bound in cloth) in the year of the Heber sale. It describes 4326 items, only

---

[1] Huntington bought the E. D. Church, Beverly Chew, F. R. Halsey and Bridgewater House libraries entire, as well as important sections of many more.

[2] Largely unpublished. A transcript is in the collection of Mr Ray L. Murphy of New York.

one of which, a manuscript, cost over £100. The *incunabula*, of which there are a fair number, were seldom important enough to exceed £5, and the majority of the books are English literature, biography and the like. Pickering's taste for 'moderns' is shown by Keats's *Endymion* in boards at 9s., four Shelley firsts, topped by *The Cenci* in calf at 18s., Lamb's *Specimens of the English Dramatic Poets* in calf at 12s., and three Byrons, the quarto *Childe Harold* in boards costing 6s. But compare this last with £10 for the ten-volume collected edition of Byron, 1822–5, in half morocco. The only first edition from the whole of eighteenth-century prose literature, catalogued as such, is a copy of Johnson's *Journey to the Western Islands* at 10s. 6d., though for poetry there are solitary titles of Collins, Cowper and Gray. Earlier centuries fare a little better. The 1532 *Chaucer*, a fine copy, costs £21, Spenser's *Colin Clout* £3. 3s. and Herrick's *Hesperides*, described as 'rare', £2. 12s. 6d.; Webster's *White Devil* and *The Duchess of Malfy* are 6s. each, while Donne, another favourite of Pickering's, has three first editions, with the *Poems* at 10s. 6d.

These humble spring blooms are put quite in the shade by the representatives of the prevailing taste. Homer runs to 21 items, Horace to 40, Walton (with no first *Angler*) to 30, while Bewick occupies two whole pages. The original edition of Shakespeare's *Poems* (1640), admitted to be 'scarce', is priced at 18s.: but Pickering's own little reprint of 1826 costs £4. 4s., because the plates are on india paper. Haslewood's 1813 edition of Painter's *Palace of Pleasure*, printed on vellum, is £31. 10s., and those far too familiar acquaintances of the modern catalogue-reader, Worlidge's *Gems* and Lodge's *Portraits of Illustrious Persons* occupy places of honour at £10. 10s. and £35 respectively.

It is, in short, clear that even a bookseller prophetic enough to list as first editions a number of books highly prized today had to accommodate his opinion, as expressed in his prices, to contemporary taste.

The Corser and Daniel sales in the sixties seemed to a later observer[1] to be 'the starting point of a new epoch'. In the sense

[1] Hazlitt, op. cit., p. 272.

that they marked a substantial rise in prices since the Heber sale and a heightened collecting activity, this was perhaps so: certainly, the latter saw the first appearance of Huth, a major figure of the next generation, as a heavy buyer. But in fuller perspective they seem rather to be points, though significant ones, in the upward curve of the purely literary criterion in collecting taste.

It must not be supposed, because emphasis is placed here on the early stirrings of that sort of book-collecting which has been of dominant interest in the past fifty years, that tastes of an earlier origin were not cultivated alongside the later, just as they are today. We need only recall the names of the Earl of Ashburnham and of R. S. Holford, whose library, formed in the years after 1840, has been described [1] as 'an exact replica of the *Bibliotheca Grenvilliana*'. But in the two countries with which we are concerned collectors of early printed books in the Roxburghe-Spencer-Dibdin manner became gradually fewer in relation to the whole (but of course progressively increasing) body: a decline perhaps not unconnected with the inroads of more 'practical' subjects on the study of latin and greek.

Across the Atlantic this broad evolution of taste was later in beginning and slower in taking hold: and it comes as a shock to realise that of the fifty principal collectors' libraries in New York in 1860 less than half a dozen contained any Shakespeare at all. [2] But if this retarded development was to some extent due to the tenacity of traditions inherited originally from England, it mainly resulted from the paramount position occupied in the collecting world of the United States during the middle years of the century by the devotion to Americana.

The two giants of the period were James Lenox of New York and John Carter Brown of Providence, whose collections, though by no means restricted [3] to, were certainly dominated by, their

---

[1] De Ricci, *English Collectors*, p. 116.

[2] James Wynne, *Private Libraries of New York* (New York, 1860).

[3] Lenox, for instance, was described in Quaritch's *Dictionary of Book-Collectors* (1896) as 'the greatest Bible collector of his age'.

Americana; and though a Thomas P. Barton might collect Shakespeare or a George Ticknor Spanish and Portuguese books, for every one collector who followed some similarly individual bent there were ten dedicated to the prevailing taste, often to the exclusion of almost all others.

One individualist may be singled out as a portent of what was to come. Charles W. Frederickson [1] of New York was collecting Shelley first editions, books from the libraries of Lamb and Byron, and literary manuscripts, at a date when such conduct must have been labelled as eccentric by even the charitably minded among his peers. But the very fact that his enthusiasms seem ordinary enough today marks him as a pioneer. Earlier in date and equally prophetic, though here in technique rather than in his objectives (which were fine MSS. and early printing), was Henry Perkins, a London brewer, who has been marked down [2] as perhaps the first to carry out, and with conspicuous skill, the 'cabinet' theory of book-collecting. This trend away from large-scale, wide-ranging collections, of whatever general character, was due partly to the increasing prices of books, partly to shrinking house-room; but partly also, I suspect, to a definite movement of taste. Largely unconscious in England, this was rationalised into a sort of philosophy by a group of contemporary French collectors who, reacting from what they rudely called *les bibliophiles de la vieille roche*, prided themselves on a sort of microcosmic elegance, an ability to express a refined eclecticism within the confines of a single book-case. [3]

These two trends, the one of taste the other of technique, were soon to meet in Frederick Locker (afterwards Locker-Lampson), whose Rowfant Library, while not by any means the most important, was possibly the most revolutionary in its influence upon following generations that the whole century produced. For Locker 'formed in two small book-cases such a gathering of first

---

[1] Cf. Granniss, 'American Book Collecting', in *The Book in America* (New York, 1939), p. 317, and Harry B. Smith, 'Gentlemen of the Old School', in *The Colophon*, no. 3.

[2] Pollard, loc. cit.

[3] Cf. the preface to the catalogue of the Henri Beraldi collection (1892).

editions of English imaginative literature that the mere catalogue of it (printed in 1886) [1] produced the effect of a stately and picturesque procession. Some of the book-hoards of previous generations could have spared the equivalent of the Locker collection without seeming noticeably the poorer, but the compactness and unity of this small collection, in which every book appears to have been bought for a special reason and to form an integral part of the whole, gave it an artistic individuality which was a pleasant triumph for its owner, and excited so much interest among American admirers of Mr Locker's poetry that it may be said to have set a fashion. [2]

This was indeed the 'cabinet collection' *par excellence*, for Locker's field embraced English literature from Chaucer to Swinburne. It set others thinking besides American admirers of *London Lyrics*, as we shall see in the next chapter. It also marked, though it did not perhaps initiate, the emergence of a factor which bulks so large in modern bibliophily that the layman may be excused for equating, as he is apt to do, the part with the whole: viz. the overriding importance attached to chronological priority— first edition, first issue, etc.—as a criterion of the interest of a book. This now preponderant factor is actually of quite modern development, for the average nineteenth-century collector was as much interested in the finest-looking or the best-edited edition as in the first. And some good judges,[3] who regard this exclusive elevation of the first edition as a very parochial limitation on the health and growth of bibliophily, believe also that it will be transitory. Whether this proves to be the case or not, we need to remember that chronological priority is only one of many criteria in book-collecting. But it has been an increasingly dominant one during the past seventy-five years, so that its influence is of necessity taken for granted in the pages which follow.

[1] An Appendix was added in 1900.
[2] Pollard, loc. cit.
[3] Among them Mr E. P. Goldschmidt, from whom I have borrowed a phrase or two in this paragraph.

CHAPTER II

NEW IDEAS AND NEW METHODS

Time which antiquates Antiquities, and hath an art to make dust of all things, hath yet spared these minor Monuments.

SIR THOMAS BROWNE

THE collecting of early printed books, fine bindings and the masterpieces of typography and illustration of all periods continued strongly during the last quarter of the nineteenth century, as it continues today. It was nourished by a series of important dispersals of libraries of the Roxburghe period, several of which had been kept intact by entail until the Cairns Acts of the early eighties. The Beckford and Hamilton sales of 1882–3, the Sunderland (Blenheim) Library, 1881–3, the Syston Park Library, formed by two generations of earlier Thorolds, 1884, and the Ashburnham sales of 1897–8 (this last a library of later formation but in the Roxburghe tradition) provided a continuously rich hunting-ground, of which the great Bernard Quaritch was chief ranger. To collectors like William Morris or C. Fairfax Murray or George Dunn, early printed books, whether or not accompanied by early MSS., were a field in themselves. To Henry Huth or Robert Hoe, probably the two most important collectors of the second half of the century, they were a part, though an important part, of a wider prospect. For these two, the one an Englishman, the other an American, found time, money and enthusiasm not only for *incunabula* and Caxtons, but for first and early editions of English literature from Chaucer to Shelley; and if Huth's collection of Americana was remarkable for an Englishman, so for an American was Hoe's of French literature and illustrated books. This catholicity of scope, this grand manner in book-collecting, has had its representatives in later generations—J. P. Morgan, Henry Huntington, Sir Leicester Harmsworth and their like. But if it needed to be said[1] at the turn of the century that 'those who

[1] Hazlitt, op. cit., p. 341.

buy books in the United States are by no means all Hoes and Morgans', it is equally necessary to distinguish in retrospect those significant developments of collecting taste which were going on alongside, and largely independent of, these major campaigns. For it was not only a difference in the length of the purse that dictated the difference of approach.

The conception behind the Rowfant Library had many attractions, not only for the new generation of American collectors in search of new ideas, but also for Locker's fellow-countrymen, among whom the library of B. B. MacGeorge of Glasgow, though it was not as much publicised at the time,[1] was probably equally influential—it was certainly uncannily prophetic of future tastes. It was not merely the idea of a calculated eclecticism which appealed to collectors whose inclination or modest means made them averse from the inclusive approach; it was also the attention given to modern authors. Here the ground had already been prepared, in respect of the Romantics,[2] by one or two pioneers—collectors like Frederickson, booksellers like Pickering the younger, who was listing Tennyson first editions as early as 1870. And by the eighties the time seemed ripe for attacking authors even nearer in date. There was already a keen school of collectors of Dickens and Thackeray, overlapping, but beginning to be distinguishable from, the more numerous collectors of Cruikshank, Phiz and other illustrators, who could not wholly ignore the authors attached to their favourites. Ruskin Societies were springing up all over England, and Browning Societies too, as those who still read J. K. Stephen will remember.[3] Wordsworth and Shelley Societies were founded in London. And this close, enthusiastic study of contemporary or nearly contemporary authors' lives and works engendered an atmosphere in which anyone prone to book-collecting or already a collector of something else passed very easily from study of the author to the search for his original editions. As early as the seventies Harry Buxton Forman had been producing private reprints of Shelley's *rariora*, in approximate type-facsimile style,

[1] A catalogue was printed in 1906.
[2] *Adonais* fetched £25 at auction in 1875, £42 in 1878.
[3] 'There's a Me Society down at Cambridge' (*Lapsus Calami*).

and the Shelley Society, under Wise's impetus, developed this provocative activity still further in the following decade.

The cult for moderns, for such it soon became, expanded with feverish rapidity during the last fifteen years of the century. 'As the distance in time between collectors and the object of their enthusiasm lessened, their interest took on a more personal colour, and the sentimental element became gradually stronger. Collectors... paid more attention to minor productions; they visualised the arrival of the first copies on the author's breakfast-table—a powerful influence in the creation of a taste for "original condition".'[1] The main emphasis was on the poets, and though Ruskin's prose works were collected as reverently, if not as expensively, as his verse, it was not George Eliot's *Adam Bede* so much as a copy of *Brother and Sister*[2] or of *Jubal and Other Poems* on special paper which would excite her devotees. Tennyson, Ruskin and Swinburne were perhaps the reigning favourites, but Andrew Lang, Austin Dobson and even Norman Gale were eagerly sought after.

This notable development in taste was closely connected with a contemporary development in technique: the rise of the author-bibliography. In the earlier years of the century, while the collector of typography and illustrated books could consult his Hain, his Panzer and his d'Essling, the collector of English literature had practically nothing but Lowndes—a general manual of great value in 1834 and not contemptible today, but quite insufficient for the needs of collectors fifty years younger than Heber and with very different ideas. The early hand-lists[3] of modern authors, for they were little more, were the work of far-sighted professionals like Richard Herne Shepherd, with his Ruskin (1878), Dickens, Thackeray and Tennyson; or of librarians like J. P. Anderson, whose Rossetti, Scott, the Brontës, etc., were mostly printed as

---

[1] Carter and Pollard, *An Enquiry into the Nature of Certain Nineteenth-Century Pamphlets* (1934), p. 100.
[2] A forgery, cf. Carter and Pollard, op. cit.
[3] For a convenient list of these, see Michael Sadleir's article in the Bibliographical Society's *Studies in Retrospect* (1945), p. 148.

appendices to biographies; or of the enthusiasts of the literary societies—F. J. Furnivall on Browning, W. E. A. Axon on Ruskin.

Buxton Forman's *A Shelley Library*, however, was a horse of a different colour: no mere hand-list but a fully annotated and richly informative study of Shelley's original editions. Published by the Shelley Society in 1886 (the promised second part never appeared) and modestly sub-titled 'An Essay in Bibliography', Forman's book marked a radical advance, not only in its detailed technical treatment of a single author's first editions but also in its forethought for the collector's wants. For it was compiled by a scholar who was also a collector himself. Its predecessors had stimulated collecting, both by suggestion to enthusiasts who were not collectors and by providing a target of completeness at which previously desultory collectors would be encouraged to aim. They had also answered the expressed need of already keen author-collectors for something comprehensive, however bare of detail. But Forman set a wholly new standard, both for his readers and for subsequent bibliographers. His *Shelley Library* was a prototype as well as a portent.

The Forman technique was adopted, developed and amplified (sometimes unnecessarily amplified) by his disciple, Thomas J. Wise. And in appraising the character of that development and amplification it is perhaps well to remember that where Forman was both a scholar and a collector, Wise was both a collector and a dealer. With characteristic prescience and practicality he set out to provide the kind of reference book which would satisfy the needs of both fraternities. He achieved it. And he never departed from it. The formula is to all intents and purposes constant from the bibliography of Ruskin (by Smart and Wise) in 1889–93 to that of Byron in 1937. Wise was not a really good bibliographer— aside from some shortcomings of method, he lacked the essential motive: a disinterested wish to arrive at the truth—but he did provide exactly what he correctly judged the new school of collectors to need. His bibliographies and later the catalogues of his library (there is little difference between them) gave a great deal of information. They were not above mentioning prices and underlining rarities (in a few cases, as we now know, with criminally ulterior motives) and they were reassuringly dogmatic in any question of priority between issues and editions.

Wise's own very fine collection contained a great number of seventeenth- and eighteenth-century first editions, mostly plays and poetry. But his earlier bibliographical work [1] and almost all his bibliophilic propaganda were devoted to the century from 1790 to 1890. In the intervals of business he found time not only to produce bibliographies and to operate as a private dealer, but also to edit, with Robertson Nicoll, *Literary Anecdotes of the Nineteenth Century* (1895–6), a two-volume miscellany much of which was written by Forman and himself; to look after the Shelley Society, and particularly its reprint programme; to write a regular column on book sales for *The Bookman*; and to intervene in print in any newspaper discussion on the topic of 'collecting moderns'. In addition he kept up a considerable correspondence, especially with American collectors like William Harris Arnold and John H. Wrenn, so that his influence began to be as powerful in New York and Chicago as in London. His energy, indeed, was as remarkable as his foresight, skill and shrewdness.

Wise was not the only, though he was the most effective, champion of the new school. Edmund Gosse's library catalogue was printed in 1893, and contained a good show of half a dozen 'moderns'. T. B. Smart's bibliography of Matthew Arnold appeared in 1892. W. F. Prideaux was at work on Stevenson. Luther S. Livingston, who contributed a column to the New York *Post* and whose catalogues are still useful, specialised in Tennyson and Lamb. Forman was the acknowledged expert on Keats [2] and Shelley and their circle, and was publicist for the collecting of Tennyson, Morris and E. B. Browning. J. H. Slater published in 1894 his *Early Editions of Some Popular Modern Authors*, a guide to the new territory which has since been colourfully described [3] as 'the revolutionary primer' of the movement. Prices responded

---

[1] E.g. Bibliographies of Ruskin (1889–93), Swinburne and Robert Browning (1896), Tennyson (1908).

[2] Wise had announced a projected bibliography of Keats in 1884, but it was apparently abortive.

[3] Carter and Pollard, op. cit., p. 103.

sharply to the growing demand, and often achieved publicity which added fuel to the flames. For while it was hardly news that Shakespeare or Milton first editions should fetch money, it was quite something that a collector could be found to pay £50 for a book by Tennyson or Ruskin, and more than £500 for the Kilmarnock Burns. Neither were such collectors lacking nor did such prices fail to be approved rather than condemned by the bibliographical expert of *The Bookman*.

There were, however, a number of conservatives to pour cold water on what William Roberts[1] called 'the First Edition Mania' and to play Cassandra to the prices it evoked. 'The craze for first editions', wrote Roberts, 'is not by any means a recent one, although it may be said to have now reached its extremest form of childishness. Time was when the craze existed in a perfectly rational form, and when the first editions in demand were books of importance and books with both histories and reputations, whilst their collectors were scholars and men of judgment. Now, every little volume of drivelling verse becomes an object of more or less hazardous speculation, and the book market itself a stock exchange in miniature.' And it is indeed recorded[2] that, perhaps for the first time in history, the booksellers hoarded first editions of Browning's *Asolando* on publication day (in December 1889) for an expected rise. Another and a more considerable dissenter was W. Carew Hazlitt, whose *obiter dicta* have several times been quoted in these pages. For many years the adviser of Henry Huth and the compiler of those *Collections and Notes* on early English books which were the first serious attempt to supplement and amplify Lowndes, Hazlitt represented the old school of collecting in its most finely crusted form. And as it is very necessary that the 'modern' movement should not assume, merely because it was a violent movement, too great an importance in our review of this period, I propose to print here, as a corrective, Hazlitt's list[3] of

[1] *The Fortnightly Review*, March 1894.
[2] Pollard, loc. cit.
[3] Op. cit., p. 60.

those subjects which, at the turn of the century, he considered 'principally engage the notice of specialists'. Here it is:

Ancient Typography
   (including Xylographic works)
English, Scotish, and Irish History
English Topography
English Genealogy and
   Family History
Liturgies and Prayer-books
Books of Hours
Bibles
Early English Poetry
Early Romances
Early Music
Spanish Romances
Italian Romances
Dantesque Literature
Cromwell Literature
Civil War and
   Commonwealth tracts
Editions of the *Imitatio Christi*

Roman Catholic Books
English Books printed abroad
Voyages and Travels
Irish Literature
Scotish Literature
Early illustrated books
Modern illustrated books
French illustrated books
Books of Emblems
Books of Engravings
Editions of the *Pilgrim's Progres*
Occult literature
Folk-lore
Tobacco
Educational books
Caricatures in book form
Miracles and phenomena
Broadsides
Chap-books

To this list, which ignores almost the whole of our national literature and thought after 'early English poetry' and 'early romances'—that is, from Shakespeare at latest onwards—Hazlitt adds the bland comment that 'there is probably not much of consequence to be suggested outside this calendar from which an intending collector may make his choice'.

This is, of course, the opposite extreme. But the fact that what would now seem to many such a thoroughly archaic list could be printed in a manual of book-collecting in the present century is a useful reminder of the tenacity of many of the tastes of the last— tastes which continued to find expression in the activities of such collectors as Lord Amherst and Lord Carysfort, as among their successors in our own time. Although the assault-troops of the modern movement had established a beachhead, there were still a surprisingly large number of books esteemed today which fifty years ago were not even in sight over the horizon.

These developments in taste were accompanied by significant developments in technique. Though the Rowfant conception of what was earlier known as the 'cabinet collection' maintained its hold on many collectors, to be revived by a later generation under the ugly slogan of the 'high-spot', author-bibliographies of the type which were becoming familiar in the nineties did more than provide information for collectors of the new school. They also influenced their method of attack. Just as the stamp album, through the power of irritation exercised by those blank squares, inculcates the desire for completeness, so also does the full-dress author-bibliography. At all times the discovery that there are still books by a favourite author not represented on his shelves will impel many a collector, sometimes with growing enthusiasm, sometimes perhaps against his better judgment, to fill every remaining gap in the list. But in the nineties in particular the lay-out of the new and exciting author-bibliographies discouraged discrimination between the more and the less important items. For there was little of the degressive principle in the treatment of their material, and the most trifling pamphlet was described as carefully and as impressively as its author's acknowledged masterpiece: indeed, the accompanying estimates of the rarity of such things tended to endow with a quite disproportionate glamour what William Roberts scornfully called 'rubbishy tracts' and 'flatulent little *biblia abiblia*'. Yet if these novelties were over-emphasised by the *avant-gardistes* of the movement, the foundations were nevertheless being laid of that principle of absolute completeness in an author-collection which has so powerfully influenced many of the most distinguished and thoughtful bibliophiles of the past fifty years.

In the second place, the much more precise descriptions of a book's exterior, as well as its interior, hastened the recognition by collectors of the desirability, if not the full significance, of original condition. Here again Wise was a pioneer, both by example and precept: for he paid record prices for boarded and wrappered copies of books which a previous generation would have preferred, if they wanted them at all, in an imposing morocco; and in his newspaper articles he never wearied of pointing out that the difference between the prices paid for copies of modern books in original state and copies rebound was not only justified but would increase. His judgment proved perfectly sound, even if his own growing influence did much to make it so.[1]

This new predilection was still, as indeed it has always remained among many collectors, chiefly a matter of sentiment—the desire for the greatest attainable degree of intact originality in an original edition; and of conscious connoisseurship—the ambition to have your books in the condition favoured by the fastidious and the expert. Eighty years earlier Dibdin[2] had written to a friend in Oxfordshire who had sought his advice on binding: 'I recommend Russia—neat, and classical, and as chaste as the nymphs that inhabit the Abingdon hills; on second thoughts, a little chaster.' But by the end of the century the pundits of the new school would have forbidden rebinding, in russia or anything else, on pain of being cut at the next Shelley Society meeting. They would have recommended a solander case for the preservation of wrappers, boards, and before long of cloth too. That this change in technique was not founded on, and was for some years seldom allied with, any true appreciation of the bibliographical and technical importance of original condition is sufficiently evident from its restriction to books from about 1790 onwards. Wise thought no more than a chronic rebinder like Huth of putting his seventeenth- and eighteenth-century books into morocco and gilt edges, unless they happened, as with some eighteenth-century poetry, to have survived in wrappers, or plain stitched, and uncut. Little if any

---

[1] Despite his public pronouncements, Wise remained a realist, recognising that in some instances fidelity to the principle of original condition might be more trouble than it was worth. For instance, he wrote to John H. Wrenn in 1903 as follows: 'To attempt to collect Scott completely in fine original state, boards sound and labels intact, is practically an impossibility in one lifetime, even if cost were to be altogether disregarded....I could point out to you half-a-dozen men who have been collecting Scott for many years, and are still far from finality, only because they have been trying to collect him in "pristine condition" all through.' (*Letters of Thomas J. Wise to John Henry Wrenn*, ed. Ratchford, New York, 1944, p. 328.)

Wise lived to see Hansard Watt, William van Antwerp and Morris L. Parrish (and perhaps others) prove him wrong in this particular instance; but that does not rob his advice of common sense.

[2] Letter to James Swann, 17 October 1817, quoted by N. Orwin Rush in *Imprimatur*, vol. 1, no. 1 (1946), p. 5.

attention was paid to the 'original' quality of vellum or calf or marbled boards with calf backs as the standard or 'trade' (i.e. the equivalent of publisher's) bindings of the books of earlier centuries. Yet whatever the motives of its recognition, the importance of original condition became one of the tenets of the new school of collectors of 'moderns', and it was a potent legacy to the following generation.

CHAPTER III

ASHBURNHAM TO BRITWELL

The Huntsmen are up in *America*.   SIR THOMAS BROWNE

THE drums and tramplings of the modern school and the dust of controversy which they evoked in some quarters had little effect on the steady development of book-collecting in other well-established departments. The Grolier Club was founded in New York in 1884, with Robert Hoe as its first President. It was by constitution dedicated largely to the appreciation and encouragement of fine book-production and of the graphic arts: but the strain of pure bibliophily was strong from the first, and as time went on it produced notable fruit. In London, the Bibliographical Society was founded in 1893. Its purpose, productions and general atmosphere were, and have remained, strictly technical: but technique's influence on taste is at least as powerful as the interaction in the opposite direction (some examples of which we have already noted), and the need for up-to-date tools had become pressing among collectors of *incunabula* and early English books.

The study of early typography had made steady progress since the days of Hain. But it was Robert Proctor, following and developing the tradition of Henry Bradshaw, who effected, at the turn of the century, a revolution in the bibliography of *incunabula* which gave a more discriminating, more scholarly turn to the collector's enthusiasm. The connoisseurs had of course well appreciated the distinction in importance and rarity between the lively products of the 1460's and the prolific but too often tedious output of the 1490's. They had distinguished between fine and mediocre printing; and their perhaps immoderate admiration for Nicholas Jenson testified at least to a recognition of superiorities in type-design, even if a high regard for the Aldine greek showed the ascendancy of traditional esteem over sound judgment. But even if mere priority to the magic (and quite arbitrary) date of 1500 had endowed all *incunabula* with a general *cachet*, the influence of more acute bibliographical and typographical studies was soon visible among the collectors of early printing between 1890 and 1920. 'Proctor's order' may have seemed to the dilettanti among them to savour more of the Code Napoléon than the Pax Augusta: but it was rapidly apparent that its injunctions were absolute and would not be (as they have not been) rescinded.

Similarly, in the field of Americana the prodigious researches of Harrisse, of Sabin, of Wilberforce Eames brought a new order into a field of bibliographical scholarship pioneered by Obadiah Rich and Henry Stevens, the great bookseller-experts, and by the earlier collectors—James Lenox, John Carter Brown, George Brinley, Charles C. Kalbfleisch and their successors. And here again the comprehensive assembly, accurate arrangement and scholarly exposition of a large body of widely popular material not only opened new horizons to succeeding generations of bibliophiles but powerfully influenced contemporary taste as well as tactics.

In early English literature, it seems extraordinary in retrospect that Lowndes [1] had not merely held the field from 1834 to the end of the century but had actually been for most of that time almost alone in it. Yet on reflexion it is perhaps not so extraordinary after all. Lytton Strachey said [2] of Gibbon that 'the material with which he had to cope was still just not too voluminous to be digested by a single competent mind. In the following century even a Gibbon would have collapsed under the accumulated mass of knowledge at his disposal.' Lowndes was no Gibbon: but his compilation was undertaken at a similarly fortunate moment in the development of bibliographical knowledge. The subsequently accumulating mass has effectively daunted any aspiring successor, and Lowndes was the first and last man to attempt singlehanded a bibliographical manual for the whole of English literature. Later (and often better) men have had to restrict their field, leaving such a comprehensive task as the *Cambridge Bibliography of English Literature* to a whole team of experts.

During the middle years of the century much valuable use, it is true, was constantly made of the sale catalogues of great libraries.

[1] *The Bibliographer's Manual of English Literature* (4 vol., 1834).
Portraits in Miniature (1931), p. 161.

32

Lowndes's *Manual* itself was revised by H. G. Bohn in the fifties,[1] though the result was no great improvement on the original. Hazlitt's *Handbook* (1867) and *Collections and Notes* (1876–1903) provided a vast number of collations and descriptions of early English books, even if they are confusingly arranged and often inaccurate. Thomas Corser's catalogue of his library, the *Collectanea Anglo-Poetica* (11 vols., 1860–83) preserved, as de Ricci[2] says, 'much information not available elsewhere'. And these were not the only supplements to Lowndes.

But it was only in 1880, when Henry Huth's great five-volume catalogue appeared, that a really substantial advance in method was registered. For although as a reference book this work is inevitably restricted to the contents of a single library, however rich, Huth (with F. S. Ellis, the bookseller, and Hazlitt, his advisory bibliographer) gave full titles and full collations, both of which were innovations in a catalogue of this kind, and innovations of the utmost significance. The Huth catalogues not only set a precedent for future collectors, so that others have followed him in enriching our reference shelves as well as recording the contents of their libraries. They set a target for bibliographers too. And if for the period between 1640 and 1700 we are still largely dependent[3] on catalogues of individual collections—from Church (1909) to Pforzheimer (1940)—the *Catalogue of Original and Early Editions...from Langland to Prior*, that admirable compilation of a group of anonymous bibliographers of the Grolier Club, published in four volumes between 1893 and 1905, is only one, though an early one, of a number of bibliographical reference books to show the influence of the standards set by Huth.

The bibliographical attack on English books before 1640 in general—the *STC* period, as we have now learned to call it—and on Shakespeare and the Elizabethan dramatists in particular, was led by A. W. Pollard, E. Gordon Duff, Falconer Madan, R. B. McKerrow, and W. W. Greg. All pillars of the

---

[1] 11 vol., 1858–64.   [2] Op. cit., p. 151.
[3] The groundwork at least will have been laid with the completion of Mr Donald Wing's continuation of *STC* to 1700 (New York, The Index Society, in progress).

Bibliographical Society, all previous incumbents of the Sandars chair, in which the very recital of their names causes me to tremble as I sit, these men worked closely together, bringing to bear on the complicated problems of their chosen period a co-ordinated volume of talent and devotion such as no single generation in the history of bibliographical scholarship had ever seen or is ever likely to see again.

It was against such a background of bibliographical research that the collectors of the end of the last and the early years of this century prosecuted their various operations. And it was now that the Americans began to assume that preponderance, in the field of English literature at any rate, which they have in general maintained ever since. Here only Sir Leicester Harmsworth, Wise (on a restricted scale, though with great shrewdness), and a small handful of others held their own. In other or in more specialised areas certain English collectors retained at least the initiative, as they continue to do today, by virtue of foresight, expertise or pertinacity—witness such recent dispersals as the Schwerdt collection of sporting books, the John Meade Falkner library, Thorn-Drury's unrivalled Restoration library, or the still intact Dexter collection of Dickens. But the earlier formula, of the English 'milor' accumulating pictures, *objets d'art* or books as a natural by-product of his grand tour of Europe, was now reversed. It was the Americans' turn to claim their share of a common literary heritage. And if some of them brought to the quest more enthusiasm, sentiment and money than knowledge or connoisseurship, it is an all too common reaction of vexation and envy to magnify these into a majority. Even if this had ever been true, we should still, as Dr Chapman has well put it,[1] be 'constrained to admit that the Americans have taken what they have taken not only because they are richer, but also because they wanted it more than we wanted it; and that many of our recent losses [he was speaking in 1930] are due not to poverty but to indifference'. But that it was not true even in the period of the great American invasion of our sale-rooms

[1] Op cit., p. 62.

and bookshops—a movement as spontaneous and irresistible as their country's expansion into its own western territories a few generations earlier—is demonstrated by a mere citation of the names of such serious and knowledgeable collectors of the time as Church, White and Clark, Palmer, Hagen and Halsey, Clements and Chapin, Harry Widener and Beverly Chew.[1] The keenness and enterprise of these men were backed, of course, by long purses: but America is hardly to be blamed if book-collecting seemed (and still seems) a natural and respected activity of the rich, who in our own country mostly preferred (and still prefer) to spend their money on other things.

Above the heads of even this commanding assemblage towered the three great figures of Folger, Morgan and Huntington. The first was the most specialised, though Shakespeare and Shakespeariana collected on Folger's scale produced an 'author-collection' larger than many general libraries. The second, notwithstanding very fine literary manuscripts and some attention to first editions, excelled particularly in the perennially stately departments of early printing and illustration, of illuminated and calligraphic MSS. Huntington, the third of the trio, set himself perhaps the most ambitious task of all: to provide the Pacific coast with a library which should not only rival the riches of the older institutions of the eastern seaboard but should put San Marino in the same class as London, Oxford and Cambridge. All three men became magnets for the attraction of likely books from dealers and private owners throughout the world. But if Folger and Morgan were better known to the English public, the one from his single-minded purpose, the other from his prominence in other than bibliophilic fields, Huntington was the most formidable rival to collectors of English literature. For his scope was as all-embracing as his energy and funds were inexhaustible; and through his redoubtable agent, the New York bookseller George D. Smith, he dominated, as perhaps no other single collector has done before or since, a whole series of sales of outstanding importance—among them Huth, Hoe and Britwell. The Britwell Library dispersal was spread over nearly twenty

[1] The brief best sketch of American book-collecting known to me is that of Ruth Granniss, contributed to *The Book in America* (New York, Bowker, 1939).

years (from 1908) and more than twenty sales, as befitted 'the greatest collection of old English books ever brought together by a private individual'.[1] And Huntington now, like its founder at the Heber sale eighty years before, grasped his great opportunity.[2] His resolution was no doubt sharpened by the knowledge, not merely that no similar opportunity was likely to occur in his lifetime, but that no library remained at all in England in private hands whence, from a single source, he could lay so much of the foundation for the edifice he had in mind.

Meanwhile, as the third generation of American collectors succeeded the second, New York had seen its first sale of a library of international stature. The Hoe collection was sold in 1911–12, just as the sales of his contemporary Henry Huth's collection (1911–22) began in London. There had been plenty of substantial American sales in the previous century; but the successful disposal of a world-famous collection in New York rather than in London was significant of the preponderance now established in the international book market by the American collector.

Equally significant of the coming-of-age of the American collector in matters of taste was the increasing evidence of an interest in his own literature. We have noted that the mid-century pioneers were much preoccupied with what is called *Americana*, i.e. books about America, early American printing, etc. But just as readers in the United States continued for many years after 1776 to regard English writers more highly than their own countrymen, so had the collectors, as they turned to literary first editions, turned first to English authors, modern as well as ancient. The Lewis and Clark of the new movement were the Leon Brothers, whose now celebrated catalogue of American literary first editions was issued as far back as 1885. P. K. Foley, also a bookseller, has been[3] ac-

[1] De Ricci, op. cit., p. 113.

[2] He bought the Americana section *en bloc*, after it had been catalogued but before it came up for auction.

[3] By David Randall and Michael Papantonio in *The Publishers' Weekly* (New York), 21 February 1931.

corded 'the mantle that in England is worn by Lowndes' for his book *American Authors 1795–1895* (New York, 1897). William Harris Arnold, Herschel V. Jones and Beverly Chew, among their other collecting activities, had all paid some attention to American authors before the turn of the century, and so had that scholarly bookseller, Luther S. Livingston. W. A. White and Owen F. Aldis, whose collections are now at Harvard and Yale respectively, were even more significant figures. But the outstanding specialists prior to the great awakening of the twenties were J. Chester Chamberlain (sale 1909) and Stephen H. Wakeman (sale 1924). Indeed, by the teens the movement was noticeable across the Atlantic, and the London *Book-Prices Current* shows a respectable number of entries for the members of the 'Cambridge school'. Even Poe and Hawthorne were not yet fetching big prices by today's standards. But the first editions of a fair number of American writers were now firmly if modestly established in collecting favour.

The broad development of collectors' tastes among the first editions of English literature during the first twenty years of this century was marked by no such fluctuations as had disturbed the two previous decades. It was, rather, a period of consolidation. As Messrs Roberts, Hazlitt *et al.* had predicted, there was a recession from the feverish popularity of the 'moderns': but it was by no means so powerful as they had expected and hoped. The prices of Tennyson, Swinburne and Ruskin dropped somewhat, the passion for pamphlets was less universal among the new school, the Romantics levelled off a little—in short, a sense of proportion reasserted itself in the obvious places. But it was nevertheless clear that certain principles had been established and had survived the early excesses. Growing attention continued to be given to original condition in nineteenth-century books. Association copies were increasingly prized. And, most important of all to the historian of taste, modern and even contemporary authors could now be collected without the suspicion of faddism or eccentricity.

The eighteenth century was still, comparatively, neglected. Indeed, it is one of the oddest phenomena in the history of bibliophily that collectors of first editions, having started, perhaps naturally, with the earlier authors, should have turned next to the nineteenth century, leaving the eighteenth, except for a handful of conspicuous books, in a semi-darkness which was to be fully illuminated only in the nineteen-twenties. The number of entries for an author or a book in *Book-Prices Current* gives some idea of contemporary turnover, and thence to some extent of demand, though the statistics can be extremely misleading unless they are used with great caution and a full allowance for such invisible factors as rarity. Yet some tentative deductions can be drawn from a comparison of the index volume for 1887–96 with that for 1907–16. We find, for example, that the space occupied by Bewick, Dickens and Ruskin has shrunk, while Blake, the Brontës, Donne and Milton have expanded. As an example of the continuing preference, among collectors of nineteenth-century first editions, for poetry over prose (the Brontës were an exception, thanks partly to Wise's championship) it may be noted that Trollope was represented in the earlier decade by *only three entries*. Even in the later he had achieved no more than half a column: less than 10 per cent of Swinburne.

Author-bibliographies, as we have seen, seldom march far out of step with the progress of collecting taste; and their evidence adds some telling strokes to the general outline of the picture. Between 1900 and the beginning of the First World War bibliographies, of varying degrees of elaboration, were published of such nineteenth-century authors as Tennyson, Stevenson, Lamb, Byron, Scott, Meredith, Coleridge, de Quincey, Fitzgerald, Ruskin, Thomas Moore and Austin Dobson. But of earlier authors we find Donne and Johnson, done thoroughly; Swift, Goldsmith and Sheridan, done after a fashion; a check-list of Dryden's plays, Trent's canonical list of Defoe; and hardly anything else. Northup's *Gray* followed in 1917, but for author-bibliographies of other eighteenth-century figures the world was content to wait—indeed, for several is still waiting.

A more precise index to the fashionable taste of this period is provided by a book published just at the beginning of the next. Seymour de Ricci's 648-page volume, *The Book Collector's Guide*

(Philadelphia, 1921), is subtitled 'A Practical Handbook of British and American Bibliography'; and justly, for as well as providing a good deal of miscellaneous information in handlist form, together with auction records and price estimates, it also directs its readers to those author-bibliographies and library catalogues in which they may find more details. But its professed object was to list 'the two or three thousand British and American books which fashion has decided are the most desirable for the up-to-date collector'.

We shall return later to the question of fashions in collecting, and the *table d'hôte* menu for collectors. In the present context we gratefully recognise that de Ricci, a sort of *condottiere* operating on the frontiers between bibliography and bookselling, was a shrewd and experienced observer of the collecting world and therefore well fitted to give a faithful account of prevailing tastes. For his bibliographical details he drew freely and avowedly on the available authorities; and if he was apt to give fuller space to an author for whom particulars lay readily to hand than to one who involved any spade-work, the mere fact that the former had already received authoritative attention elsewhere was a fair enough reflexion of his current rating.

De Ricci's *Guide* is an endlessly instructive work for the student of evolution in collecting taste. But we must here restrict ourselves to a handful of examples, in the field of literary first editions, of the difference in emphasis between 1921 and 1949. We shall note, then, that Donne has 7 entries and Swift 4, while Edward Ravenscroft and John Crowne, two Restoration dramatists of no excessive stature, have 12 and 18 respectively. Samuel Johnson rates 6 entries to Thomas D'Urfey's 29. Thackeray occupies nine pages with 50 entries; but neither Trollope nor Wilkie Collins appears at all, and Mrs Gaskell is represented only by *Cranford*—and not the first edition (1853) at that, but the first illustrated of 1860, included because a presentation copy had fetched 'the fancy price of £31 at Manchester' in 1914. Among more modern prose writers, Stevenson runs to 84 entries, while Hardy, although two bibliographies of his works had appeared in 1916, scores only 4. Among American authors a stark, and perhaps not wholly representative, comparison is provided by Longfellow, with 52 entries, and Fenimore Cooper, who gets a three-line note. 'Most of his first editions', de Ricci points out, 'may be obtained at about $4–$5 apiece. Even *The Last of the Mohicans*...seldom brings more than $15–$20. These low prices [he sapiently concludes] should not last long.' The prophecy was amply justified. Yet de Ricci, with the Chamberlain sale twelve years behind him and the Wakeman sale only three years ahead, reflected so conservative a view of American literature that he gave Riley and Field only one entry apiece, and omitted Charles Brockden Brown and Herman Melville altogether.

If de Ricci's sceptical treatment of several now popular American authors, in a guide published by an American firm, suggests that this branch of collecting was still, in the eyes of an international observer, working its passage to full recognition, his estimates of comparative importance among the Victorians are equally revealing. The eighteenth century is certainly somewhat better thought of than it had been twenty years earlier: but its treatment would have seemed derisory six or eight years later. A good deal of attention is given to sporting books and colour-plate books and to the illustrations of Rowlandson and his school, the taste for which was long-established and persistent, as, with some fluctuations in the price-range, it has since remained. But as for the classics of economics, philosophy or politics, let alone those of science or medicine, they clearly had no place at all among 'the two or three thousand books which fashion has decided are the most desirable for the up-to-date collector'. For Newton, Berkeley, Blackstone, Hume and Darwin do not rate a single entry between them; and while Albert Richard Smith, the author of *Christopher Tadpole*, is allotted 32 titles, his namesake Adam is not mentioned at all.

Temperamentally de Ricci perhaps belonged to an earlier age of taste, as Hazlitt did when he wrote his collector's manual a generation earlier. But he was professionally adaptable, not opinionated, like Hazlitt; and if his heart was with Rothschild or Pichon he had applied his great abilities and his wide experience to the needs of those 'up-to-date' collectors whom he was addressing. Yet in the light of the developments of the next quarter of a century some parts of his *Guide* look today hardly less antediluvian, in their implied estimates of relative importance, than Hazlitt's list of 1904, quoted above, would have looked to de Ricci and his contemporaries. Revolutionary changes were due—perhaps overdue: and indeed the roaring twenties were only just round the corner.

CHAPTER IV

BUXTON FORMAN TO KERN

Deus quos vult perdere, dementat prius.   JOSHUA BARNES(?)

THE period between the end of the First World War and the great world slump of 1929–30 was marked, in the smaller world of book-collecting, by a number of explosive features analogous, in their psychology if not always in their direction, to the economic, political and social upheavals of that strange decade. Collecting had continued briskly during the war: but the few developments of taste had remained unpublicised and were consequently limited in their impact. Even the repercussions normally set up by significant sales had been muted by the noise of events, though in fact most of the major dispersals of the period—the later Huth and middle Britwell sales, the Mostyn plays, the Fairfax Murray *incunabula* and others—were remarkable for grandeur, not for originality.

The influence of an important sale on bibliophily at large is twofold. It is apt to produce a number of high prices, which attract public notice. This enhances the stature of the pursuit and occasionally recruits adherents, as well as bringing to light other copies of the same books. But it also affects the thinking of collectors themselves. It is true that in the electric atmosphere of a great sale a few books fetch prices which look ridiculous twenty years later: as Hazlitt [1] said, 'it is not merely the article which has to be considered, but the atmosphere in which it was sold'. And if we are reminded of the Valdarfer *Boccaccio* in the Roxburghe sale in 1812, plenty of similar freak records could be quoted for our own generation. On the other hand, Wise [2] once observed, apropos Shelley's *Original Poetry by Victor and Cazire* (1810), which had fetched £600 at auction in 1903, that 'a market price has now been made for the book, and experience shows that for books of

[1] Op. cit., p. 290.
[2] *Letters to Wrenn*, ed. Ratchford (New York, 1944), p. 335.

the first order of rarity the price invariably goes forward'. And de Ricci[1] said: 'When a book has once sold for an enormous price and another copy turns up unexpectedly, the price of the new example is always strongly influenced by the former record. Such fancy prices are not, as many people believe, sporadic instances of an individual collector's excitement, but have in many cases a permanent influence on the book-market of the world.' This thesis would be the better for some serious qualifications,[2] but it contains a great deal of hard truth. We remember that the Syston Park copy of the *42-line Bible* cost Quaritch £3900 in 1884, but only £2950 in 1898, when it reappeared in the Makellar sale. On the other hand, the Newcastle copy of Audubon's *Birds of America* fetched £2400 in 1937, which was a 50 per cent advance over previous levels and was widely regarded at the time as a fancy price. But the book has never since sold publicly for less.

The second and more important influence exerted by the sale of any collection, whatever its magnitude, which has been formed with taste, judgment and (especially) foresight, is simply that of example. For unless its composition had previously been made familiar to the collecting world by means of a catalogue, it will be seen for the first time in its entirety, by all but those friends or scholars who have had privileged access to it, on the shelves and in the catalogue of the auctioneer.[3] Mere sheep-like imitation is not in question; but there are few collectors so complacent that they are not glad to pick up a hint or two from a fellow-expert, whether in matters of method or of choice. And few would not admit to some advantage, often unconsciously drawn, from the study of the connoisseurship of another, as displayed in his books. There were several such sales during this period, and their influence on the taste of other collectors can be seen in retrospect to have had a permanent quality quite distinct from any temporary contribution to the graph of general enthusiasm and rising prices.

[1] *Guide*, p. xii.   [2] See, for example, p. 15, above.
[3] The reverse is also true. Collections which change hands privately *en bloc* are deprived of the influence which public dispersal would have given them; though they may exert it by prior (e.g. Rowfant) or subsequent (e.g. Halsey) cataloguing.

The last decade of the previous period had been impressively marked by three major dispersals: the sales of the incomparable Britwell Library, formed in the early middle of the nineteenth century, and of the two greatest collections of its second half, formed by Huth and Hoe.[1] The post-war decade was ushered in by the sale of the first really important collection formed by a leader of the succeeding generation, that 'modern school' of the late nineteenth century on which his influence at the time had been, as we have already noted, so powerful. Harry Buxton Forman had been a very shrewd as well as a scholarly collector. He was a pioneer in his taste for the Romantic poets and nineteenth-century writers; he was a pioneer in the bibliographical exposition of his favourites; and he was also a pioneer in one particular technique of acquisition very well suited to his main field and extensively developed since. In the course of his researches into the lives and works of Keats and Shelley, he had made the acquaintance of their descendants and their friends' descendants. And he had found opportunities of purchasing from some of these persons rarities and association material of a kind which, under normal conditions, would have come into the market slowly, belatedly and piecemeal, if at all. His example had been followed by Wise and Clement Shorter, who traced and acquired considerable quantities of Brontë and Borrow material, particularly manuscripts; and the technique was classically demonstrated in Wise's capture, after a pertinacious siege, of almost the entire contents of 'No. 2, The Pines'. It was *a fortiori* applicable, and has been very widely applied, not only by collectors but by institutional librarians, to the works of authors still living and tolerant, if nothing more, of a bibliophilic Boswell. Here again the pattern was set by Locker and Wise with Browning, Wise with Conrad, Forman with William Morris.

The Buxton Forman sales in 1920 were not remarkable only for the impetus they gave, both by the example of a well-rounded pattern and the opportunity of purchase, to the collecting of the Romantics and nineteenth-century writers, especially the poets. They were held in New York, not London, the collection having

[1] The Britwell and Huth sales continued into the twenties, but their style and content were characteristic of the previous era.

been bought *en bloc* from the heirs:[1] and this was taken, as it was doubtless intended by those who promoted the sales, as a challenge to the primacy of London in the disposal of literary collections of this kind. Incidentally, these sales provided the first salient opportunity for a trial of strength between the *diadochi* to the empire of George D. Smith, whose commanding position in the American book trade had been terminated only by death.

Four years later was sold the equally rich and more catholic library of Bernard B. MacGeorge, whose influence on the *cognoscenti* of the Locker and post-Locker school of collecting had also been strong. Now, almost two generations later (a bibliophilic generation may be reckoned at twenty years), MacGeorge's excellent judgment, nice regard for condition and remarkable prescience made a second and equally sharp impact on the taste of the twenties. The Shorter and Gosse collections were not in the MacGeorge class. But their dispersals, also in London but later in the decade, were well timed to reinforce existing trends. In Gosse's case the effect was not only felt among collectors of nineteenth-century authors, though prices were very high in that department. His Restoration dramatists were also considerable and his eighteenth-century books not negligible.

Sales of such collections as Clawson's (New York, 1926) of Elizabethan and Stuart literature, or Holford's (London, 1927–8) of early printing and early English books, were of course more important than these, in the sense that a picture dealer calls a picture 'important' because it is a large and a fine example of the master's familiar manner. Furthermore, in any decade or in any year, there are sales of libraries from country houses which make valuable—sometimes sensational—contribution to the flow of books through the market. But these are more often accumulations than

---

[1] By John B. Stetson, whom the owners believed to be a private collector. But the library was thereupon put up for auction at the Anderson Galleries; and the fact that a facsimile of Buxton Forman's bookplate was made for insertion in those books which had none renders it difficult to refute the belief (entertained by, among others, Mr Maurice Buxton Forman and the London firm who valued the library for probate) that material was added which had never belonged to the collector under whose auspicious name it was sold.

collections: formed either haphazardly through the centuries, or in a single period when some literary squire interrupted a regular line of fox-hunters and bought books as they came out. Such libraries seldom reflect the taste of an earlier bibliophile, so they do not, except by accident, affect the taste of later ones. We are here concerned with influence, not with casual abundance nor even with magnificence on established lines.

Two sales held in 1924, however, both in New York, were influential in two fields of collecting which were just then in an interesting stage of development. The Wakeman sale of American first editions came at a time when, as the result of the labours of earlier experts, that fascinating though bibliographically stony field was ready to bear a real crop. Wakeman's fine collection aroused intense interest in the auction room, and many of the books realised prices which, if they seem modest enough today, were remarkable then. In consequence, whereas those already collecting American literature were heartily encouraged, many of their countrymen, who had been too busy in other directions to consider it as more than a side-line, sat up sharply and began to take notice. With the Wakeman sale American first editions attained their full majority as a department of bibliophily: one which has gained steadily in stature ever since, so that today Poe is as expensive as any English author this side of 1700.

The second significant sale was that of John Quinn, who had been the Maecenas of many contemporary writers, particularly English writers. He had also collected their books and manuscripts with a generous enthusiasm and had eventually amassed an almost exclusively modern library of a kind which had never been publicly dispersed before. The authors who were 'modern' to the revolutionaries of the nineties had remained in varying degrees of favour, but the collecting taste of succeeding decades had not kept them up-to-date by any notable infusions of fresh blood. Few people in the teens collected Dowson or Yeats, Henry James or Walter Pater, let alone Marie Corelli or Conan Doyle, though Kipling headed a small group of exceptions. Now, however, with that cyclic character which bibliophily shares with other tastes, the time was ripe for a new attack on the new moderns. The Quinn sale was the starter's pistol, even though a handful of far-sighted specialists were already out of sight beyond the second or third jump.

The vogue for collecting contemporary English authors was the most conspicuous, though the least important, of the developments of the twenties. In contrast to the predilections of the nineties, prose took the lead over verse, and the popularity early achieved by Conrad and Hudson was soon overtaken by Barrie, Galsworthy, and Shaw. American collectors were as keen as English; indeed, keener; and it was noticeable that though a certain sympathetic increase was registered in their interest in contemporary American writers, from Theodore Dreiser to Edna St Vincent Millay, these were mercifully spared the worst excesses visited on the Europeans. It was also noticeable that among the contemporary British authors of an eminence likely to attract the less enterprising collectors, fashion dictated with its usual brusquerie. Norman Douglas was fashionable, Max Beerbohm was not (nor, quite inexplicably, ever has been). *Ulysses* (Paris, 1922) was unsaleable at 10 per cent of the price of *My Lady Nicotine* (1890). Galsworthy's earliest and least interesting books were extravagantly esteemed, but Wells and Arnold Bennett (save for one book) went a-begging. There was a brisk vogue for D. H. Lawrence and A. E. Coppard: Virginia Woolf and E. M. Forster were ignored.

I have used the word 'fashion' advisedly. For if it was true that Wise and his friends set fashions in the nineties, they went about it consciously, with conviction and care. But the great herd-movements which swept to and fro, unshepherded, across the twenties were of a different order of blinkerdom as well as of mere size. There is always an agreeable element of uncertainty in collecting contemporary writers: for a man must back his fancy, and only his grandchildren will know whether posterity's verdict looks like confirming or confounding it. In theory, therefore, it is ideal ground for the novice, encouraging individuality and minimising expenditure. And so, in general, it often is in practice. But so in the twenties it most emphatically was not. The authors on whom attention was mostly concentrated were all well established in the esteem of the reading public, and collectors dully, obediently and every year more expensively followed suit. It was of course a period of generally rising prices, especially in America. Book-collecting had for various reasons come to be regarded as 'the done thing' among many persons desirous of being thought cultured. And without the restraints which discrimination, connoisseurship and individuality of taste impose on true bibliophily, the result was .an undignified stampede. No wonder Mr Shaw was quoted[1] as saying: 'One begins, naturally, by plundering the collectors, who never read anything.'

The effect of these violent concentrations of demand on a com-paratively narrow area was exacerbated by a breezy disregard of comparative rarity among the books concerned. Experienced collectors move very warily in new territory, for there are always exceptions to even such plausible expectations as may be founded on previous observation of similar ground. But most of these now on the war-path were not experienced collectors. On the contrary, they were only too prone to believe, on the analogy of the stock-market, that because a copy of *Plays Pleasant and Unpleasant* (2 vols., 1898) or of *Jocelyn* (1898) by 'John Sinjohn' had cost £50 last year and was now offered for £75, it was as certain as that the sun would rise that its price next year would be £100. Nor were the book-sellers, whose general, if not special, experience should have warned them of these dangers, sufficiently resolute to deny their impetuous customers or put a curb on sky-rocketing prices. There were, needless to say, sober spirits, genuine individualists, knowledgeable veterans among the crowded ranks of the collectors of moderns. But neither they by example nor the more sceptical dealers by precept had any appreciable effect on the enthusiasts. Too many of these were 'suckers' of the purest vintage, and where there are suckers there will be exploiters and speculators. Nor were such wanting, mostly in that ambiguous no man's land between the trade and the collector, where part-time dealers and amateur book-sellers flourish in times of confusion.

[1] By A. J. A. Symons, in *The Book-Collector's Quarterly*, no. 1 (1930), p. 46.

The same airy optimism, the same jettisoning of well-tested safety precautions characterised the later stages of another and a far more important development of the twenties. If the pleasure of collecting 'moderns' had been rediscovered after a period or inattention, the eighteenth century, as a whole and for the majority, was being discovered for the first time. We have noted earlier its strange neglect by previous generations of collectors and the few, though gradually increasing, exceptions to that neglect. Some attention, it is true, had for years been paid to certain outstanding books and authors. The 1887–96 index to *Book-Prices Current* shows a turnover of eleven copies of Boswell's *Johnson*, though the average price (excluding extra-illustrated copies) was only £1. 12s. In the 1907–16 index Fielding occupies a whole column. Blake, for pictorial rather than literary reasons, was by exception a well-established favourite. Wise and some others had been steadily buying the poets and dramatists. There were a number of specialists, like R. B. Adam, Harold Williams and the youthful W. S. Lewis. Nor must we forget the influence, on collectors as well as readers, of such literary critics as George Saintsbury and Leslie Stephen, Edmund Gosse and Lytton Strachey; of such books as Cross's *Fielding* and Austin Dobson's *Eighteenth-Century Vignettes*. But we have seen how little of the eighteenth century de Ricci prescribed for the 'up-to-date' in 1921; and it would probably be fair to say that even an ambitious eclectic collector of English literature in the early twenties would have considered few additions necessary to the twenty-six titles which represented (and very judiciously) the eighteenth century in the Grolier Club's classic exhibition of *One Hundred Books Famous in English Literature*, held twenty years before.

But just as the less obvious Victorian fiction was due for discovery, and later, with some assistance from a few devotees, achieved it, so was the eighteenth century—indeed, long overdue. And although there had been preliminary mutterings and isolated excursions, it is tempting, and I think justifiable, to assign a precise date to the effective beginning of what was to become within five years one of the widest and deepest movements of taste in the whole history of bibliophily. *A Catalogue of Books by or relating to Dr Johnson and Members of his Circle* was issued by Elkin Mathews, Ltd., the London booksellers, in 1925. 'This catalogue', Mr W. S. Lewis[1] recently declared, 'is a milestone in the history of bookselling, for in it appeared books priced from ten shillings to two guineas which had never appeared in any West End catalogue before.'[2] This was not the first catalogue of the newly revived firm but the fifth, nor was A. W. Evans its only director, for he had learned and lively colleagues.[3] But here was the considered manifesto of a new movement in bibliophilic taste; and if its bibliographical harbinger was Iolo Williams's *Seven Eighteenth-Century Bibliographies*, which had appeared in the previous year, Evans was without question its prophet. 'In his shop,' says Mr Lewis again, 'the eighteenth century was the sole reality.' This could be said without disparagement to those other firms of booksellers, such as Pickering and Chatto or Birrell and Garnett (under Graham Pollard), who were already catering expertly to eighteenth-century specialists, and without overlooking the preparatory influence of Everard Meynell. Evans had been a scholar and critic before he turned bookseller: it was this which lent persuasive authority to his zeal: and it was zeal which the newcomer could throw into the scale to balance the seasoned experience, the detailed knowledge of the actual books of the period, of dealers like Charles Massey (who died in 1928) and Mr Percy Dobell. Evans showed an instant grasp of two means—now very well recognised, but then innovations—by which a catalogue could exert influence over those collectors not within immediate reach of his silver tongue and studiously informal shelves. He dignified a book in which he believed by pricing it according to his view of its deserts, regardless of its current rating, if any, elsewhere: and having caught the reader's eye, he added a critical note if he thought the book needed it. Both practices rapidly became characteristic of the firm's catalogues, in which the eighteenth century was always prominent. Indeed, 'blurbs' from

[1] 'The Bookseller as Teacher', in *The Atlantic Monthly* (Boston), February, 1947.

[2] This is actually an exaggeration, as reference to a file of Pickering and Chatto catalogues, for instance, would show.

[3] In particular the Hon. R. E. Gathorne-Hardy: Greville Worthington and Percy H. Muir joined the firm later.

Hazlitt or Matthew Arnold, originally culled by Evans and his partners to justify a high price for some neglected masterpiece, turn up in other booksellers' catalogues to this day.

Evans's campaign for the eighteenth century could not have succeeded if the time had not been ripe. On the other hand, no such campaign, planned in a bookshop, would have had so immediate and striking an effect without the Elkin Mathews combination of scholarship and showmanship, of imagination and shrewdness behind it. Their influence was direct, on their private customers and on institutional libraries of sympathetic tastes. It was also indirect, through other London booksellers who recognised a good lead when they saw it and followed suit, and through American dealers who bought from Evans or applied his precepts to other shelves. Elsewhere, the cosy volumes of A. Edward Newton, a fanatical Johnsonian, spread the message to his large following, while such books as A. S. Collins's *Authorship in the Days of Johnson*, such learned propagandists as R. W. Chapman, appealed to the more sophisticated. Within a very short space of time the boom in the eighteenth century was running as strongly, both in the auction room and in private trading, as the boom in 'moderns'. Since it had previously been (except for a small number [1] of individual books) the poets who stood out from the comparative obscurity shrouding the period, so it was now the novelists, essayists and other prose writers who rose in favour even more sharply than Pope and Gay. Boswell's *Johnson* and *Tom Jones* were soon in three figures; the large paper *Gulliver* in four; and when every allowance has been made for the general increase in book prices between 1920 and 1929, some of the records set by Goldsmith, Smollett, Fanny Burney and even the smaller fry in the latter part of the decade make fantastic reading today.

The intensity with which the 'moderns' and the eighteenth century were now cultivated was matched by certain exaggerations of method. Among the collectors of 'moderns' only the

[1] E.g. *Robinson Crusoe, Gulliver's Travels, The Vicar of Wakefield, Tristram Shandy, Evelina.*

lunatic fringe pushed the pursuit of 'mint' condition to the point where dust-jackets were considered a matter of serious concern. But the manufacturers of points and issues drove a thriving trade. The mechanics of modern book-production proved to be almost as prolific of bibliographical complexity as the resettings and cancel leaves which bedevil seventeenth- and eighteenth-century books; and the very fact that the results seemed beneath the notice of the established experts of the earlier period—were, indeed, quite out of sight of a good *STC* man—inspired a kind of defiant affection among the devotees of 'moderns'. Many a distinction of state or issue in a twentieth-century book is perfectly valid, as fuller investigation and calmer reflexion have established. But in the heyday of the twenties calm was at a discount and 'points' at a premium, so that no fashionable first edition was thought complete without an early date on the inserted advertisements, a misprint or two, or at least a broken letter, whether significant or not.

The boom in the eighteenth century was accompanied by a technical fallacy of a different kind, but one equally mischievous in its indiscriminate application. Respect for original condition was by now an article of faith with all serious collectors, no matter whether the book in question were Donne's *Poems* (1633) or *King Solomon's Mines* (1885). But while this will be generally approved as a notable development in connoisseurship by our present standards, some of the eighteenth-century enthusiasts of the twenties carried it to an extreme point from which, unfortunately, it has not even now recovered. For they found that although the first purchasers on publication day of *Roderick Random* (2 vols., 1748) or *Yorick's Letters to Eliza* (1773) would have been handed volumes bound in original trade calf (the contemporary equivalent of publisher's cloth), there did also occasionally survive copies in wrappers, or in boards. These relics of the chrysalis stage in eighteenth-century book-production, of the status of which I shall have more to say in a later chapter, were now elevated to a wholly disproportionate degree of esteem relative to copies of the same book in original calf. Collectors who had learned that leather-bound copies of *The Woman in White* (3 vols., 1860) or *Poems and Ballads* (1866) had no place on self-respecting shelves were encouraged to apply the false analogy to *Moll Flanders* (1721) or *The Task* (1785): and, in a now notorious instance, the spurious glamour attached to what was advertised as the only known copy of *Tom Jones* (6 vols., 1749) in the original boards, uncut, so dazzled a series of professional experts that they failed to note that twelve of its leaves had been supplied from the second edition.[1]

The revival of attention to contemporary writers was a conspicuous, and the discovery of the eighteenth century a notable, development of collecting taste. But they were both movements within the general framework of the established taste for first editions of English literature, the gradual evolution of which during nearly a century we have cursorily reviewed. Another development initiated in the twenties, which made much less noise at the time, was nevertheless of a quite different order of importance: it was in fact a revolutionary departure from all the accepted canons. This development may be roughly defined as the recognition that thought is as worthy of the *general* collector's attention as imagination.

Such a conception was less of a novelty to Continental bibliophiles. More than half a century earlier that remarkable character Guglielmo Libri, whose rascalities have unduly obscured his talents, had included in his very catholic library a number of important scientific books and manuscripts. But when some of these (e.g. Kepler) were sold in London in 1859 their reception showed that Libri was far in advance of English taste. There had been, of course, specialist collectors of scientific books in England, even if the greatest names are Continental—Falconet, Michel Chasles, Duhem, Prince Buoncompagni. Moreover, such men as J. R.

---

[1] The Jerome Kern-Anderson Galleries-Rosenbach-Owen D. Young-Gabriel Wells-Rothschild copy, the defects of which were exposed by Mr John Hayward in 1940. Lord Rothschild's suit (U.S. District Court, Southern District of New York, Civil Action 17/210) for recovery of the purchase price was eventually settled out of court in 1944, in the plaintiff's favour.

McCulloch, the historian of political economy, had formed collections to which, while they were perhaps still primarily 'working libraries', had been applied some of the connoisseurship that distinguishes the collector from the practical accumulator. 'I have seldom neglected', wrote McCulloch in the preface to the catalogue[1] of his library, 'any opportunities, of which I could avail myself, to substitute superior for the inferior copies of books in my possession.'

More recent and more directly contributory to the coming change of attitude in the general collector were the activities of such scholarly but essentially bibliophilic specialists as Sir William Osler. In his great collection of medical literature he gave positions of equal honour to William Harvey's *De Motu Cordis* (Frankfort, 1628) and Sir Thomas Browne's *Religio Medici* (1642) and sought the best available[2] copies of both. Osler was indeed the prototype of the humane specialist. His particular brand of bibliophily, carried on and developed by his pupil and biographer, the great and beloved Harvey Cushing, and spread across America by graduates of the Harvard and Yale Medical Schools, has probably begotten more distinguished special collections than can be credited to any one man in the whole history of book-collecting. In England, Lord Keynes directed a similar attack on the broad but hitherto neglected history of English thought; and he was not the only prophet.

Yet if Osler's disciples applied strictly bibliophilic and bibliographical standards to the collecting of medical and scientific writers, this was still a far cry from the equating *by the general collector* of the first edition of a scientific or philosophical work with its contemporaries in the field of pure literature—the *Discours de la Méthode* (Leyden, 1637) with *The Duchess of Malfy* (1623), Kant's *Critik der reinen Vernunft* (Riga, 1781) with Johnson's *Lives of the Poets* (4 vols., 1781) or *Tract Ninety* (1841) with *The Dream of Gerontius* (1866). And it was in the later twenties that such

---

[1] Privately printed in 1846. The passage is quoted in full in Quaritch's *Contributions towards a Dictionary of Book Collectors*, part 6.

[2] Of the former he eventually had to conclude that 'good copies...do not exist'.

a proposition was first deliberately advanced. Again, the impregnating factor emanated from a bookshop, and again that bookshop was Elkin Mathews. If the firm's championship of the eighteenth century was founded on the temperamental Johnsonianism of Evans, the impulse to this much more drastic innovation was generated in the thoughtful unconventionality of approach to the business of bookselling which was the hallmark of these inspired amateurs and their enduring contribution to the always important part played by the trade in the development of collecting philosophy. Since specialist collectors had for years been buying the original editions of Vesalius or Hume, Spinoza or Ricardo, Linnaeus or Clerk Maxwell, so the specialist booksellers had been stocking and cataloguing them. But they regarded such books, quite justifiably in view of prevailing attitudes towards them, as being of strictly technical appeal; and they were priced and described accordingly. The now celebrated series of catalogues issued between the years 1906 and 1920 by Henry Sotheran and Co. under the title *Bibliotheca Chemico-Mathematica* were, indeed, edited (by a pioneer scholar in this field, Mr Zeitlinger) with a fullness of description which perhaps recognised that others besides specialists might be tempted by their contents. But it was Messrs Elkin Mathews who deliberately selected books of historical significance in the fields of science, philosophy, economics and politics for inclusion *as equals* among first editions of fiction, poetry and the drama. They priced and promoted them as equals: and whether implicitly by mere juxtaposition or explicitly by a forcible note, they advertised the conviction that such books had an unquestionable right to the serious attention of the general collector.

This imaginative extension of the sum total of potentially collectible books found a ready response. If the established specialists complained at the prospect of an invasion of their preserves by the multitude, it was nevertheless both gratifying and encouraging to see Hunter's *Treatise on the Venereal Disease* (1786) or Malthus's *Principle of Population* (1798), Boyle's *Sceptical Chymist* (1661) or Newton's *Optics* (1704) rising in price in response to a wider demand. Thoughtful collectors were grateful for the pointer to unfamiliar but well-stocked territories, into which they might escape from the expanding pressures and spiralling prices or an overcrowded and ever more shrilly exploited market. Beginners who felt, with some excuse, that many first editions of English literature were now almost out of reach of the modest purse, saw rewarding possibilities in the exploration of hitherto neglected shelves.

The giddy atmosphere of book-collecting in the later twenties lent an unhealthy intensity to any and every development in taste. Growing-pains there inevitably were, but they were not felt till the following decade.[1] Among the many disciples of Dr Pangloss, the few voices of caution were no more effective than Cassandra's. Of the four considerable developments we have noted, two survived substantially intact the over-stimulation to which they were immediately subjected. The advance of American first editions was to continue unchecked, partly because it was confined to one continent and so halved its liability to hysteria, but mainly because it was no more than the logical and consistent intensification of a steady trend and therefore escaped the excesses which beset innovations. The acceptance by others than specialists of the products of human thought—the landmarks of civilisation and progress as distinct from the masterpieces of literature—was more than confirmed during the following decades. There were some natural and healthy revaluations in the popularity (and thence in the price) of a dozen or two of its most obvious and therefore first exploited representatives, which either turned out to be commoner than had been expected or were seen on maturer reflexion to be less cardinal to their respective subjects than early enthusiasm had supposed. But this radical innovation appealed first to intelligent collectors rather than to the majority and therefore developed in a comparatively orderly manner. Moreover, its claim on their attention, however belatedly recognised, was too obviously well

[1] For example, Elkin Mathews's distinguished catalogue of *Byron and Byroniana*, the product of a keen attention to this author, had been preparing before the slump. But it was not issued till 1930, and its failure did as much to kill the boom in Byron as the firm's previous efforts had done to promote it.

founded to be much affected by the intemperate habit of the time.

But the general inflation of prices and the gusts of fashion; the lack of discrimination between the more and the less important books, and between the rare and the common books in either category; and finally a financially speculative tendency among collectors as well as dealers—such a combination held the seeds of disaster not only for the comparatively fragile vogue for a handful of popular contemporary writers but even for the soundly based and responsibly supported invasion of the eighteenth century. For this too became 'the fashion', and consequently fell liable to fashion's instability.

The great boom of the twenties culminated in the sale of Jerome Kern's library in New York during the winter of 1928–9. This resplendent, if somewhat gaudy, collection, assembled in no more than fifteen years, dramatically epitomised the popular taste of the twenties in the field of English literature. Except for the conventional Shakespeares, Kern had not attempted the Elizabethans, and his American first editions were of secondary importance; but his coverage of the eighteenth and nineteenth centuries was impressive both in quantity and quality, and the collection was rich in association copies. Its sale was the most widely publicised, the most theatrical, and the most resoundingly successful ever held, before or since. It set many records which have stood to this day and its average per lot, about £240, has never been equalled. The twenties had been a period of fireworks. The Kern sale was the last big bang before the lights went out.

CHAPTER V

DEPRESSION AND REVIVAL

In the case of every artificial furore the good, bad, and indifferent are apt to rise and to fall together, while it is reserved only for the first to experience a revival. W. CAREW HAZLITT

THE intensity of limited enthusiasms and the general curve of prices had increased during the later twenties with the sharpness of an arithmetical progression. In face of every evidence of over-expansion and inflation, the graph of business in the book-market continued unchecked on a course which was by no coincidence parallel to that of the stock-market. And with the stock-market it collapsed. Collectors of the investment-minded kind had their paper profits wiped out inside a few months. Others of more authentic temper were sadder and wiser, if no poorer. Painful and depressing as this was at the time, it was a much-needed purgative to many genuine but misguided enthusiasts. And if the playboys, speculators and *arrivistes* who had invaded the market betook themselves elsewhere, bibliophily was well rid of them. In the chilly light of 1931–2 the compensations looked small, but they were there.

On the debit side it was seen that the departments which had boomed highest slumped hardest: the fashionable moderns and the fashionable but commoner books of the eighteenth century. It could not be foreseen then, though it is plain in retrospect, that both had gone down for a very long count indeed. Only late in the thirties did a number of really considerable eighteenth-century first editions—books like Goldsmith's *The Deserted Village* (1770), Sterne's *Sentimental Journey* (2 vols., 1768) or Burke's *Reflections on the Revolution in France* (1790)—creep back from 20 to 40 per cent of their 1929 figures. Indeed, over a much wider area the reaction was so violent that it was almost sufficient for a book to have fetched a very high price in the Kern sale to be now dispraised and rejected. For the relapse was as indiscriminate as the fever which bred it, and books both important and rare sank along with those usurpers of these qualities which were belatedly seen not to possess them. As for the half-dozen contemporary authors who had so lately been the rage, nearly twenty years were to pass before a selected few of their books returned, almost furtively, to favour. To take a single example: Galsworthy's *The Man of Property* (1906), not a rare book, but much scarcer in fine state than many that had been touted as rarities, used to sell for well over £100 in the late twenties. Even very presentable copies receded to almost single figures in the early thirties, along with commoner and much less important titles by the same author. It has since risen, slowly and still not very far, in response to the considered recognition that its merits had been unfairly obscured by boom-slump conditions and unworthy company. During this whole time it had been no less and perhaps more of a favourite with the reading public. It had been no less and perhaps more difficult to find in fine condition. It had simply been a victim of fashionable exploitation.

As the book-market began to recover from its hangover, during which, as usual, everything looked equally jaundiced, a number of general and a number of particular tendencies were discernible. Some collectors had learned the hard way that personal taste and conviction were surer guides than fashion. Some of these, again, had learned that discrimination and common sense in the practical application of taste provided a touchstone for the rules and regulations of the issue-mongers, the shrill cries of the mint-condition fetichists, and the profundities of certain dubious bibliographical manuals, mostly devoted to the moderns, which had blossomed so luxuriantly in the hot-house atmosphere of the boom and which continued to appear in the thirties. So to the faithful band of prudent and experienced collectors who had avoided the holocaust were added a number of others who, though burned, did not dread the fire but rather had learned to handle it, if not with confidence, at least with circumspection.

But, as in all spheres of human activity in times of apparent disaster and gloom, there were many collectors whom bitter experience persuaded that they had been led, rather than had simply gone, astray. And those who, crying that they have been betrayed, seek a changed and a firmer authority often get authoritarianism instead. Since devotion to a whole period or a whole category of collecting seemed to end in tears, it was tempting to suppose that salvation lay either in a single impeccably charted course (such as an author-collection), or in a classically regulated eclecticism. The *cabinet choisi* of a Beraldi or a Locker had been a reaction against inclusiveness: but it was based on individual discrimination. What the lost souls of the thirties wanted was not free will but dogma.

The richer among them, more particularly in America, found it in such canonised lists as the Grolier Club's *Hundred Famous Books*: an admirable selection, but in such a context marmoreal rather than stimulating. Those who specialised in fiction relied on A. Edward Newton's list of 'One Hundred Good Novels':[1] a purely personal choice and labelled as such, but destined to achieve a mischievous infallibility. American specialists could fall back on Merle Johnson's *High Spots of American Literature*.[2] These were only a few, though characteristic and influential, examples of the ready-made selection for book-collectors, of which de Ricci's *Guide* was an ampler specimen. Books recommended for this kind of collector went under the label of 'high-spots' or sometimes 'key books', terms as ugly in themselves as they were invitations to misuse. John Ford's *The Broken Heart* (1633) may be a better play than his *'Tis Pitty Shee's a Whore* (1633). *Ask Mamma* (1858) may be a better story than *Mr Sponge's Sporting Tour* (1853). *The Golden Bowl* (2 vols., New York, 1904) may be a better novel than *The Wings of the Dove* (New York, 1902). But the haloes thus bestowed on them cast altogether disproportionate shadows on their neighbours.

Those who still wanted moderns turned hopefully to the still increasing crop of bibliographies and hand-lists, many of them compiled either by well-meaning incompetents or by brazen exploiters. There had been a number of excellent and scrupulous bibliographies of modern authors, from 'Stuart Mason's' *Oscar Wilde* (1914) to Marrot's *Galsworthy* (1929). Nor were worthy

[1] In *This Book-Collecting Game* (Boston, 1928).
[2] New York, 1929.

successors wanting in the thirties, such as Simmons's *Masefield*, not to mention Percy H. Muir's hard-headed and cogently argued scrap-books, *Points* and *Points, Second Series*. But a number of their contemporaries did bibliophily little service and its votaries some damage to their pockets and more to their bibliographical standards.

Two periodicals bravely started at the beginning of the decade to cater to the needs and pleasure of bibliophiles: *The Book-Collector's Quarterly* in London and *The Colophon* in New York. Both printed articles of permanent value as well as of more ephemeral interest and if the former had a more consistent editorial policy, both had an influence which was healthy as well as stimulating. Equally characteristic of thoughtful bibliophily in London was the Bibliographia Series, edited by Michael Sadleir and initiated by his own pioneer study of a neglected aspect of book-production, *The Evolution of Publishers' Binding Styles* (1930). The volumes in this series—studies in eighteenth- and nineteenth-century bibliography, bibliographies proper of Scott and Beckford—were all marked by a scholarly appreciation of the importance of book-structure and publishing practice to the intelligent collector, whose acquiescence in this proposition was enlisted by being taken for granted.

Two of the volumes in the series, I. R. Brussel's *Anglo-American First Editions*, made the first serious attack [1] on the tangle of trans-atlantic priorities among the popular but uncopyright authors of the nineteenth century, which was by now giving conscientious collectors a good deal of trouble. This was a major stroke in a discussion which raged intermittently throughout the thirties and was commonly known as the 'follow the flag' controversy: the question at issue being whether the collector should prefer the first edition of a book wherever printed and whether authorised or not, or the first edition published in his native country. Logic demanded the former, even if the difference in time, as with *Huckleberry Finn* (London and Hartford, 1884) was only nine days. Sentiment clung to the latter, while cheerfully making exceptions for *Utopia* (Louvain, 1516; London, 1551) or *Adonais* (Pisa, 1821; Cambridge, 1829). Lord Esher was one influential collector who supported,

---

[1] Percy H. Muir's pioneer essay had appeared in *New Paths in Book-Collecting* (1934).

both by precept and example, the view that first means first and cannot mean anything else. But when his extensive range of (American) first editions of nineteenth-century English authors were sold in 1946, their reception suggested that the sentimentalists have gained at least a temporary ascendancy over the logicians.

In the matter of scope as opposed to taste and of strategy as distinct from tactics, the most far-reaching development of the thirties was the now apparent decline in the number of private collectors who would (or could) combine, as Huth, Hoe and Huntington had done, the inclusive approach with operation on a really massive scale. 'The days of the general library are past', wrote de Ricci in 1930.[1] And it was true. Sir Leicester Harmsworth was in his last lap. Wise had completed his great catalogue, and though he filled gaps and improved copies he hardly extended his scope during the ten years before his death in 1937. Major J. R. Abbey's expansionist period was still in the future. Harry Widener, who promised to be such a collector, had been cut off in his prime twenty years before, like Marcellus, to whom Gosse compared him. In America W. T. H. Howe, Mr Carl H. Pforzheimer and Mr Arthur A. Houghton indeed remained, with perhaps one or two more such as Mr J. K. Lilly, Jr; and if Frank Hogan's failing health had not cut short his brief period of intense and broadening activity, he might have joined them. But times had changed. The most ambitious collector of early English literature had some excuse for feeling, with Sir Thomas Browne, that the great mutations of the world were over. And functions which had been regularly performed by private collectors a hundred years earlier were now being assumed by the institutional, and especially the university, libraries of America, in whose custody already reposed so large a proportion of the fruit of those collectors' labours.

But if the tendency (and it was a rational one) was either towards eclecticism or towards specialisation on a period or a subject, on a group of authors or a single author, by no means all collectors had been content to follow existing sign-posts. Mr Albert Ehrman's

[1] 'Book-Collecting for all purses', in *The Colophon*, no. 2 (1930).

collection of early typography or Mr Lessing J. Rosenwald's illustrated books would be remarkable in any century. Among the eclectics Frank Bemis had shown what could still be done with sound judgment and fine connoisseurship backed by a long purse, while Mr Richard Jennings, on a much more modest scale, set a new standard by the combination of a sensitive palate with an extreme of delicacy in the matter of physical condition. Hugh Sharp, whose untimely death removed one of the most distinguished collectors of our time, might have moved into the widest fields, for his range was constantly increasing. But in the more selective, though very catholic, approach which actually characterised his comparatively brief collecting life, he exhibited almost to perfection the qualities of the best type of collector: strong personal likings combined with a shrewd appraisal of relative importance among the accepted great; an instinct for comparative rarities; an exacting yet rational attitude towards condition; great energy, perspicacity and business acumen; and finally a faculty of decisive action quite disproportionate to his length of experience.

Several of these qualities Sharp shared with the late Lord Keynes, who turned in his last years from a remarkable collection of the English philosophers and political thinkers to invade the literature of the seventeenth century. Here strict connoisseurship had often to yield to the determination of one who had decided that his was the last generation to whom many of these books would still be available. Time may well prove him right: and the College which he loved and to which a large part of his library was bequeathed may congratulate itself that Keynes was perhaps as far-sighted a book-collector as he was an economist.

Bibliophily is seldom hereditary. But that it can run sideways if not downwards is proved by at least one example of our own generation. Mr Geoffrey Keynes, who is better known than his brother to collectors at large on account of his prolific output of bibliographies, exerted through them a considerable influence on bibliophily in the twenties and thirties. It was not merely that his bibliographies of Blake (1921) and Jane Austen (1931) capped, at their different dates, already strongly developed tastes for those authors, while his *Donne* (1914) and his *Hazlitt* (1931) almost pioneered them. It was not merely that his *Browne* (1924) and his *Harvey* (1928), like Professor Fulton's *Boyle*,[1] added lustre as well as technical tools to the flourishing Osler-Cushing tradition. It was due also to his combination of the thorough attitude normal to an author-collection with so unusual a variety in the authors collected. This individuality of taste, with its concentration on separate areas in a wide field, offered a stimulating contrast to the eclectics on the one hand and to the specialists in a period on the other; for even if Mr Keynes has been more active in the seventeenth century than in any other, Glanville is still a far cry from Rupert Brooke and Siegfried Sassoon.

Author-specialists there have been for many years. Their contribution to bibliography and to literary history is often notable. To bibliophily it is sometimes considerable, by drawing attention to a neglected writer or showing what can be done with a well-known one; but in many cases it is definitely rather damping. 'Every collector's most intimate desire', as de Ricci[2] remarked, 'is to be in some way or other the king of the field he covers.' And few could hope to compete with—we will not say the Folger Shakespeares, but the Harmsworth Bunyans, the Ballard Kiplings, the Parrish Lewis Carrolls, the Keating Conrads; Mr Houghton's Keats, Mr Pforzheimer's Shelley, Mr Beinecke's Stevenson, Mr Howard Bliss's Hardy; Mr Keynes in Evelyn, Mr Sadleir in Marryat, Le Fanu or Disraeli, Lord Rothschild or Mr Harold Williams in Swift. Yet there were in the thirties, as there will always be, plenty of already collected authors to provide a fair field for emulation, as well as others on whom only preliminary attacks had yet been made. And if the gradual trend away from the general collection was making specialisation in a single author, or in one or two authors, rather more frequent, this was a progressive development, not an innovation.

Perhaps not an innovation but certainly a distinct and notable change in bibliophilic strategy emerged as the decade wore on:

---

[1] *Proceedings and Papers of the Oxford Bibliographical Society*, vol. III, part 1 (1932); *Addenda* in part 3 (1933); *Second Addenda* in New Series, vol. I, fasc. 1, 1948. [2] *The Colophon*, part 2.

specialisation in a period. The text-book example of this rewarding compromise between the general and the particular is probably Lord Rothschild's eighteenth-century library. Here, in little more than a dozen years' collecting, has been demonstrated that the choice of a target of a size strictly consonant not only with the available attention and means but, more significantly, with the expectable availability of material, is of fundamental importance in the planning of any collection. In the tactical area, the result also demonstrates that just as there is a right size for all things, so also is there a right time. Like Frank Hogan, who saw that the nadir of 1931 was the moment to wade in and buy Elizabethans, so Lord Rothschild was able to take advantage of that violent reaction of the majority against eighteenth-century books which followed the boom of the twenties. For some years at any rate competition would be limited; a keen buyer in a temporarily unfashionable department would get the offers; and a resolute beginning might secure foundations which ten years later would need twenty years of patient laying.

A period specialist of a different kind, whose technique as well as taste was more widely influential in the thirties, was Morris L. Parrish. Like Geoffrey Keynes he collected an author thoroughly and he collected a number of authors: but, unlike Mr Keynes's, Parrish's authors were all (except Lewis Carroll) novelists, all English, Irish or Scots, and almost all Victorians. This concentration was not a piece of considered collecting strategy. Parrish had been brought up on the Victorian novelists, he liked them better than any other reading and he collected them with a patient and increasingly skilful devotion for about forty years. The result was a library which, over the ground it covers, had only one rival anywhere, but also a library which could probably not be duplicated in another forty years' collecting by even so dedicated a collector as Parrish. It was influential in the matter of method because its owner and his exacting standards were well known to the book-sellers and collectors of both continents, and because he issued very full catalogues of several sections of it. It was probably more influential in the matter of taste because, while Parrish had been collecting Victorian novelists on a wholesale scale long before the 'minor' ones became generally popular, his reputation and his catalogues were of assistance to that popularity when it arrived.

It is important to distinguish between bibliophilic fashions and those evolutions of taste in collecting which are closely geared to the evolution of taste in reading. The Romantics have declined in popularity with collectors during the past fifteen years (Keats partially excepted) for mixed reasons. They are indeed less popular with younger readers: but their first editions are also suffering a delayed reaction from the relative over-estimation in which they were held between the Buxton Forman sale and the Kern sale, and perhaps also from the realisation that many of them are much commoner than was then supposed. There can be no doubt, however, that the long neglect of the eighteenth century as a whole by the majority of collectors was a legacy of the general distaste entertained by the Victorians for the Augustans. The time-lag between literary and bibliophilic popularity is variable, but often, as in this particular case, substantial; and it was the eighteenth century's misfortune to be discovered by collectors at large just in time to be caught up in a period of general inflation and gravely prejudiced by its aftermath. In the same way, the long neglect of Victorian fiction was a legacy of the Edwardian age's aversion from its predecessor—and shall we not soon be saying the same of those Edwardian novelists whom nobody now collects?

Among the Victorians there were, it is true, some considerable exceptions. Dickens and Thackeray had been established in collecting favour since the eighties. Meredith had enjoyed a short-lived vogue in the nineties. The Brontës and Borrow had been early publicised by Wise and his friends, and the Brontës soon outgrew the need for sponsorship: so much so that *Jane Eyre* (3 vols., 1847) was fetching £500 and £600 in the late twenties, even if Borrow was already showing signs of inability to stay the course. Isolated titles (as with the eighteenth century) had a settled esteem—*Lorna Doone* (3 vols., 1869), *The Cloister and the Hearth* (4 vols., 1861), *John Halifax, Gentleman* (3 vols., 1856). But although the pioneers had for some years been quietly collecting

Disraeli, Trollope and George Eliot, Mrs Gaskell, Wilkie Collins and the rest, these authors only came into their own as part of the general revival of Victoriana. The fact that their discovery by the main body of collectors seemed (as so often to discoverers) belated lent an additional enthusiasm very welcome in a period when the book-market was convalescent and responded briskly to a tonic. Yet neither the temporary vagaries resulting from an unhealthy concentration on the Victorian titles canonised by Newton, nor the occasional fancy prices which always accompany a public invasion of cherished preserves, should delude us into regarding as a mere fashion what was in fact the collector's expression of a much wider development in public taste.

On the other hand it would be as idle as unjust to deny full weight to the influence of those collectors and bibliographers who had pioneered the Victorian revival and now helped to chart its course. Mention has already been made of Parrish. The example of Lord Esher and Sir Hugh Walpole, the enthusiasm of Newton for Trollope and Dickens, the scholarly affections of Carroll A. Wilson—these and half a dozen more gave the movement added momentum. But to one man in particular, Mr Michael Sadleir, the collecting of Victorian fiction owed not only momentum but direction and breadth. In his bibliography of Trollope, in his *Publishers' Binding Styles*, in his studies of the fiction reprint series, even as early as his pioneer *Excursions in Victorian Bibliography* (1922), there was revealed an acute perception of that fourth dimension in collecting technique: the publishing background of the books collected. This was no novelty to the Elizabethan experts. It has since been fully explored by several bibliographers of eighteenth-century authors—Professor Pottle's *Boswell* and Miss Jane Norton's *Gibbon* are exemplary cases in point. It was also being sporadically applied in the more obvious field of contemporary writers. But it was the good fortune of those who began to collect the Victorians in the thirties that this method of approach preceded, instead of following, popular attention. Mr Sadleir's researches into the general problem of comparative rarity, his attention to book-structure and distribution methods, his analysis of the bibliography of any given book in the light of its publisher's as well as its author's temperament and practice, set a wholly new standard for collectors as well as bibliographers. Being himself an author and a publisher as well as a collector and a bibliographer, he understood very well how much the two latter have to learn about the two former. And his influence on both sides of the Atlantic has been such that the collecting of modern books in general, as well as his favourite Victorian novelists, has since been approached with a reasoned intelligence, a regard for causes as well as effects, by many collectors who would twenty years ago have considered as pedantic if not pretentious many things they now do as a matter of course. This was a development in method of profound and salutary importance.

The Second World War put a far more effective damper on book-collecting activity in England than its predecessor, so that the period covered by this chapter comes to a natural end in September 1939. Most of the ground lost in the slump had been regained, some of it more than regained. And American activity confirmed this trend until it, too, went into low gear. The developments of the past few years are still too close, and have been subject to too many abnormalities, such as the exchange control barrier between the mutually sensitive markets of London and New York, to allow of any considered analysis.

Two aspects of the English scene perhaps stand out clearly enough to be worth noting. The current boom (not yet paralleled in America) has included contemporary as well as earlier authors. On the analogy of previous periods of concentration—the nineties, the twenties—prices might have been expected to get out of hand in this always volatile department. But they have conspicuously failed to do so. And it is a welcome inference that both the trade and collectors learned their lesson last time and have not forgotten it.

The second characteristic is the tendency for the first editions of science, philosophy, economics, etc., which weathered the slump with credit unimpaired if not enhanced, to advance more steadily in popularity and more sharply in price than almost any other department of bibliophily. Some devotees of pure literature and connoisseurs of fine books affect to regard this phenomenon with impatience and even with contempt: yet if Edison and Rutherford could sit down to table with William Morris or Thomas Hardy, their first editions may surely stand without awkwardness on the same shelf. And the critics can console themselves with the reflexion that as thought never yet caught up with imagination, no more will Volta with John Keats.

CHAPTER VI

PATTERNS
IN BOOK-COLLECTING

*If the great collections of the past had not been sold, where would
I have found my books?*   ROBERT HOE

THERE are certain distinct rhythms in the history of book-
collecting, some of which have been audible in the brief
survey of the past century we have just completed. The
broadest of these has something of the sweep and regularity of the
tides: for it is part of the periodic fluctuation of literary (and to
some extent of social) taste, to which the collecting of literature in
general and literary first editions in particular must always remain
harnessed, despite any temporary or localised vagaries. The
Romantics revolted from the Age of Reason, the Victorians from
the Regency, the Nineties from the Victorians; the Elizabethan
and Jacobean dramatists were rediscovered at the beginning of the
nineteenth century, the Romantics at its end, the Victorians in our
own time; and we may confidently expect that the pattern will
repeat itself, perhaps in a modified degree and no doubt with
plenty of variations, so long as literature is read and studied. As
each tide recedes, a few more names are seen to have achieved
a secure position above high-water mark, to have become a permanent part of the average reader's landscape. Minor writers of
the same school or temper are returned, to come up again with the
next fluctuation of literary taste.

Bibliophily has its own moods and peculiarities, which qualify
its relationship to these wider evolutions. But during the comparatively short time—less, as we have seen, than a single century—
that literary criteria, expressed in terms of first editions, have been
first an important and later a dominant theme in an infinitely
varied pursuit, the relationship has always been visibly close. For
book-collecting has shown itself constantly if not always consistently responsive to each succeeding revaluation or rediscovery in

the general field of literary, historical and critical appreciation of the writers of the past. Whenever bibliophily has deserted or over-shot the common denominator between collectors and readers, as happened, for instance, in the youthful exuberance of the nineties and the indiscriminate enthusiasm of the twenties, it has paid the penalty. Collectors can be—and the good collector always tries to be—a step ahead of the literary critics. But only the most deter-mined and self-sufficient individualists can afford to be either entirely out of step, or so far ahead as to be out of sight.

A lesser but connected rhythm is observable in the book-collector's attitude to contemporary authors. A living author attracts collectors of his first editions in numbers which normally increase in proportion to his distinction and popularity, sometimes with one of these qualities, sometimes with the other in the as-cendant. If he lives to a great age, concentration tends to diminish: sometimes because his first editions become so large that they can never be scarce (e.g. Galsworthy), sometimes from a failing of his own powers or popularity (e.g. Meredith), sometimes simply because younger collectors have turned to younger writers. His death usually gives a brief fillip to the market, for it reminds us all that he will write no more. But this is commonly followed, even with the most obvious candidates for immortality, by a recession. And that recession may be long and deep, as with Kipling, or inconsiderable in either length or depth, as with Hardy. Its varia-tion, however, and the author's bibliophilic standing on his emer-gence from it, will depend on the consensus of critical literary opinion. For while a writer is alive the collector can be, and among the enterprising often is, his own literary critic. But once the writer is dead, posterity has begun. He has ceased to be a 'modern', to whom (in certain respects) a special set of collecting rules apply. He has become a unit in the history of his country's literature.

This pattern is never quite absolute in character, for the post-humous critical revaluations of any given author are seldom unanimous. Even if they were, there would always be dissenters among the collectors. Moreover, allowance must regularly be made, in this as in all other generalizations about bibliophilic taste, for that special fondness for any favourite books of our youth, from which few collectors are, or would wish to be, immune. And if this often perpetuates parental tastes or sentiments, it as often reflects the unpredictable influence of some miscellaneous shelf which the mere accident of propinquity at a receptive period has endowed with an unforgotten magic.

A rhythm of a different kind can be traced in the approach to bibliophily in general by successive generations of newcomers to book-collecting. Novices of great wealth or strongly marked predilections, or those with a clearly defined purpose and plan, are often immune from its influence. Liability to it will indeed always be in inverse ratio to the degrees of formed taste and of natural aptitude which are applied to a new pursuit. But a considerable number of persons take up book-collecting every year, and there have been certain periods when, for various reasons, recruits of rather mediocre quality have been particularly plentiful. Among them are many, perhaps even a majority, who are infected with bibliophily in a general way rather than attracted to it through some particular channel of interest. And these will be especially susceptible to the example, if not the actual precept, of others, so that they provide the raw material (or sheep) for turning any reigning fashion into a herd movement. Yet with every allowance for such influences, whose direction will vary with the taste of the time, there is a special pattern which remains constant.

Fine printing (or, in the jargon of the trade, 'press books') and modern firsts always claim a substantial share of the attention of newcomers with no firmly fixed affections. The reason is obvious: moderns provide a comparatively inexpensive proving ground for those inclined to first edition collecting, while a fine book—and sometimes, alas, even simply a pretentious book—commends itself readily to many who neither do, nor ever will, care a button for a first edition. Colour plate books and handsome (again, often showy rather than strictly fine) bindings appeal in just the same way to those whose purses are a little longer but whose first steps are equally tentative and equally liable to that necessity for justification (whether to themselves or others), freedom from which will only be achieved when the novice has ceased to be a novice.

It is therefore a very natural and a very common cycle that begins with books which please the eye, progresses to books which excite the imagination as well, and ends by eliminating conventional beauty altogether. Similarly an initial devotion to modern firsts often proves to be merely an apprenticeship for the business of attacking earlier and more difficult periods. In the latter case the collector who moves on in bibliophily, though back in time, leaves no appreciable gap in a field always fully occupied by the experienced as well as the inexperienced. But every considerable wave of new collectors has a distinct and predictable effect on the market for press books and colour-plate books, which fluctuates in response to demand with almost mathematical conformity. For since such books are born precious, since they suffer almost not at all from what the economists call 'consumption' and much less than rarer books from institutional absorption, their long-term supply is more nearly constant than that of books in any other collecting field. It is their short-term supply that varies with the periodic demand from less sophisticated or more ostentatious collectors and their subsequent extrusion when some of these turn elsewhere. Some, of course, do not turn elsewhere but develop into serious and discriminating collectors of modern fine printing. Nevertheless, as Mr Muir has acidly put it,[1] 'anyone well informed on book-collecting history could venture a shrewd guess at the state of the money-market from the current price of a Kelmscott Chaucer'.

Quite different again, largely unpredictable, but powerfully influential in bibliophilic history is the cyclic character of the opportunity of acquisition. This, in its broadest term, was put in a nutshell by Robert Hoe.[2] 'If the great collections of the past', he said, 'had not been sold, where would I have found my books?'

---

[1] *Book-Collecting as a Hobby* (1945), p. 57.
[2] Quoted by Beverly Chew in his foreword to the Hoe sale catalogue (1911).

And the motive has been explicitly recognised by such collectors as Edmond de Goncourt, who directed that his library should be sold at auction after his death in order to renew for his fellow-collectors the pleasure its assembly had given him.

But though the necessity for maintaining the general supply of rare and desirable books by redistribution becomes more evident every time a library or a special collection disappears into an institution, the cyclic element in such redistribution dates from long before institutional absorption became a serious menace and therefore invited counter-action by collectors themselves. Lord Spencer and the Marquess of Blandford saw in the Roxburghe sale an opening not to be missed. The Heber sale made an indispensable contribution to the foundations of the Britwell Library, the dispersal of which in its turn gave Huntington his chance for a tremendous *coup* in early English books and Americana. Huth and Hoe were inheritors, at only one generation's interval, from the collections of Corser, Daniel and Tite. Later in the century, the sale of a number of libraries of the Roxburghe type which had been kept intact for several generations—Beckford, Sunderland, Syston Park, Wodhull—gave a similarly non-recurrent chance to such collectors of early printing as General Brayton Ives and C. Fairfax Murray. The Buxton Forman and MacGeorge sales put every considerable first edition collector of the early twenties on tiptoe. And in a quite different department, that of American literature, Wakeman took advantage of the Chamberlain sale in 1909, to provide by his own sale in 1924 a rich opportunity for W. T. H. Howe and the other specialists of the period. Examples could be multiplied of the constant renewal of impetus given by the dispersal of carefully formed libraries to collectors of the same kind of book in the next, or even in a much later, generation. In a number of cases, of which the succession Heber-Britwell-Huntington is probably the classic example, it was more than a matter of mere impetus: it was actually that the later library could by no other means than the redistribution of the earlier have become quite what it did.[1] It is probably only occasionally, and

[1] This is neatly demonstrated by the William Beckford collections of Mr James T. Babb of New Haven and Mr Rowland Burdon-Muller of Cambridge, Mass.,

in a small area, that the collector would echo Tennyson's confession: 'how often has the choice of a rhyme helped me to a beautiful thought'. But it is certainly true that direction has been given to a collector, and the character of more than one important library influenced, if never actually formed, by a timely opportunity of acquisition.

So long as collections continue to be sold, whether before or after their owner's death and whether by auction or *en bloc* to a bookseller, rather than being given or bequeathed to a public or university library, so long will this cycle of the opportunity of acquisition perpetuate itself: and normally at intervals of about a generation. Moreover, since for half a century or more most of the big collectors have been American, its rhythm is even now more clearly perceptible in New York than in London: where, despite notable exceptions, an increasing proportion of the important sales are of libraries either of the haphazard, country-house type or, like the Clumber, Lowther, Ham House or Cunliffe collections, formed many years ago.

This tendency would only be reversed if this country regained, and held for at least a generation, the dominant position in the upper strata of bibliophily: bringing back from America a really substantial number of those important and expensive books which have been exported thither in the past. And in spite of the present (surely temporary) difference between the liveliness of the London and the apathy of the New York market, this cannot be considered a likely development. Yet, except in specifically American departments, London has hitherto always maintained some advantages of initiative in the development of collecting taste. It is still, despite the Buxton Forman or the Lothian sale, an international *entrepôt* for the collectors of both continents. And although English collectors and dealers can no longer, as they could fifty years ago, reckon to give points to the average American in connoisseurship, expertise

neither of which would have been what they are if Lord Rosebery, whose books were sold in 1933, had not been a heavy buyer at the Beckford sales of 1882–3.

or method, they can still hold their own on even terms—and still sometimes win the odd trick. But these assets will only avail to offset the economic advantages, the steadily increasing skill and the formidable energy of the Americans, if they can be not merely maintained but increased. And they can only be increased by the conscious and unremitting efforts of all four estates in the republic of bibliophily—collectors, librarians, bibliographers and book-sellers.

PART II: METHOD

CHAPTER VII

REFLEXIONS ON THE PRESENT STATE OF BOOK-COLLECTING

An editio princeps is not a mere toy—it has something in it that may purchase the attention of a thinking man.   JOHN HILL BURTON

IT is always a matter of great delicacy to discuss *how* a collector should collect, still more to discuss *what*, and still more again *why*. And even though what I have to say in the second part of this book will consist strictly of reflexions, not advice, I shall shelter behind my elders and betters at least in the preliminary examination of the last question. Mr Muir has said flatly[1] that 'the foundation of all collecting is not logical but sentimental. No self-respecting collector of books needs a reason for collecting. He collects because he likes books.' A. W. Pollard, however, laid it down[2] that 'in the modern private collection, as in the modern museum, the need for a central idea must be fully recognised. Neither the collector nor the curator can be content to keep a mere curiosity-shop. It is the collector's business to illustrate his central idea by his choice of examples, by the care with which he describes them and the skill with which they are arranged. In all these matters many amateurs rival, if they do not outstrip, the professional curators and librarians.' This has recently been reaffirmed by Mr W. S. Lewis, who wrote[3] that 'the collector's work is only partly done when he has formed his collection. Unless it is used, it is like bric-à-brac in a cabinet.' Those who have taken issue with Mr Muir's thesis see an inconsistency between these points of view. Mr Graham Pollard, for instance, maintained[4] that it 'ignores entirely the qualities in a collector that make his collecting of

---

[1] *Points* (1931), p. 3.   [2] Loc. cit.
[3] 'Collector's Progress', in *The Atlantic Monthly*, April 1947.
[4] 'Serial fiction', in *New Paths in Book-Collecting* (1934), p. 247.

importance. Critical intelligence in defining the scope of his collection, pertinacity in seeking out everything within that scope, and courage in acquiring it, all these qualities have been synthesised in the achievement of the great book-collectors.'

Mr Muir, while he may stick to his guns, would probably not dispute the doubly Pollardian thesis. Corser stands out among his contemporaries for the scholarly use to which he put his books. Buxton Forman's collecting of Keats and Shelley was essential to his editorial labours. William Morris and St John Hornby put into their own printing what they absorbed from their favourite *incunabula*. And in our own time, if *The Yale Edition of Horace Walpole's Letters* depends on Mr Lewis's sanctum at Farmington, it is equally true of *Trollope: a Commentary*, of *The Evolution of Publishers' Binding Styles* and of *Fanny by Gaslight* to say that each has its roots in Mr Sadleir's collection of original editions. Nor are those collectors necessarily any less worthy, though they may be less admirable, who have left the exploitation of purposefully assembled material to others, as Huth did to Grosart: content that the acknowledgement of their 'critical intelligence, pertinacity and courage' should be found only in the prefaces to works of scholarship. There is indeed a further stage: for the recognition that the first of these qualities at any rate is out of his reach has caused more than one eminent collector to employ an expert to advise and even purchase for him, as Huth again employed W. C. Hazlitt. Are we to say that the world of letters does not profit? Bibliophiles, certainly, will withold their applause. Yet that applause is sometimes forthcoming for a wayward or an unregulated collector: one in whom A. W. Pollard's 'central idea' seems, if not in spirit at least in execution, to dissolve into a series of eccentricities.

The generally accepted compromise over the boundary between motive and method, on the precise whereabouts of which will depend most people's decision whether the opposition of sentiment and logic is not in fact more apparent than real, is summed up in Mr Curle's conclusion[1] that 'book-collecting may not be a logical

[1] Op. cit., p. 102.

pursuit in itself, but, if we collect books, we should go logically about it'. Yet surely this solution, to which all parties would agree, is no more than 'hurrying on to safer ground'.[1] There is a real antithesis between the purely sentimental and the purely intellectual approach to collecting, and the sentimentalist will seem just as wet to the intellectual as the latter seems dry to him. In most good collectors, of course, the two ingredients of heart and head are blended, whatever the proportions in each individual synthesis. But if it is safe—and hardly necessary—to say that the collector whose prime motive is sentiment will be a better collector and have more enjoyment of his pursuit if his approach and method are intelligent (or as Mr Curle puts it, logical), it is perhaps more important, in these days of specialisation, to remember that the most expert connoisseurship, in any except a practical working collection, is a sterile thing if it is not founded on a feeling for the author or the subject or the period collected. Most veteran collectors have known the temptation to embark on some special field, far from their real interests, simply because it offers a technical attraction or even a technical challenge: just as a violinist is tempted to include some difficult but worthless piece in his repertoire for the sole reason that hardly anyone else can play it. Such excursions can be very valuable exercises for a collector, so long as they remain exercises: but whenever expertise becomes an end in itself instead of the means to an end, it results in empty virtuosity.

This and certain allied vagaries often result from a super-sophistication, a sort of finicking, a too delicate distaste for any path trodden by others. One is reminded of those critics who cannot bear to find merit in *The Pickwick Papers* or the Mona Lisa or Beethoven's Fifth Symphony simply because these are admired by οἱ πολλοί. But that they are not peculiar to an age which some think Alexandrine, is shown by John Hill Burton's[2] description of a collector of a hundred years ago.

'Let us now summon [he says] the shade of another departed victim—Fitzpatrick Smart, Esq. He too, through a long life, had been a vigilant and enthusiastic collector....He had a principle of

---

[1] Graham Pollard, loc. cit., commenting on a later passage in Mr Muir's essay.
[2] Op. cit., pp. 17–19.

selection peculiar and separate from all others', as was his own individuality from other men's. You could not classify his library according to any of the accepted nomenclatures peculiar to the initiated. He was not a black-letter man, or a tall-copyist, or an uncut man, or a rough-edge man, or an early-English-dramatist, or an Elzevirian, or a broadsider, or a pasquinader, or an old-brown-calf man, or a Grangerite, or a tawny-moroccoite, or a gilt-topper, a marbled-insider, or an editio princeps man; neither did he come under any of the more vulgar classifications of an antiquarian, or a belles-lettres, or a classical collector. There was no way of defining his peculiar walk save by his own name—it was the Fitzpatrick Smart walk. In fact, it wound itself in infinite windings through isolated spots of literary scenery, if we may so speak, in which he took a personal interest. There were historical events, bits of family history, chiefly of a tragic or a scandalous kind,—efforts of art or of literary genius on which, through some intellectual law, his mind and memory loved to dwell; and it was in reference to these that he collected. If the book were the one desired by him, no anxiety and toil, no payable price, was to be grudged for its acquisition. If the book were an inch out of his own line, it might be trampled in the mire for aught he cared, be it as rare or costly as it could be.'

Burton's list of recognised types to which his collector did *not* belong is a useful reminder that specialisation is almost as old as book-collecting. But he is chiefly concerned to illustrate individuality of taste. This essential in the book-collector's make-up has, indeed, been recommended and enjoined in almost every manual for collectors ever written, and it is extolled among the *obiter dicta* of many other authorities. 'The essence of book-collecting', as Mr Sadleir once[1] put it, 'is to want something because you yourself want it, and not because it is the kind of thing which seems in great demand.' A. J. A. Symons expressed the same idea in his comments[2] on two well-known 'blue-prints' for collectors. 'Mr Seymour de Ricci,' he wrote, 'who is a man

---

[1] 'Decentralisation or Deadlock', in *The Colophon*, part 3 (1930).

[2] 'A Book-Collector's Apology', in *The Book-Collector's Quarterly*, no. 1 (1930), p. 54.

of knowledge, published a *Book-Collector's Guide*[1] giving brief notes on the "two or three thousand British and American books which fashion has decided are the most desirable for the up-to-date collector". Could there be a more pointed, though unconscious, criticism of what is called, with appropriate ugliness, "high-spot" collecting? What is an "up-to-date" collector? As well talk of an "up-to-date" giraffe.' And again, apropos another list, which also has been mentioned[2] in an earlier chapter: 'Were Mr Newton to show me in person his hundred selected novels, no doubt they would interest me, as reflecting the peculiarities of his mind and taste; but if any other person shows me Mr Newton's hundred novels, I shall ask him why he has not made his own choice.'

These reiterations of a perennially valid principle were prompted by the distressing spectacle of those herd-movements which characterised the collecting world of the twenties. And it is natural that the re-establishment of the criteria of authentic taste should seem more urgent at times when fashion is in command or when, as in the decade following these particular warnings, disconcerted souls fall back on irreproachable respectability or the *ipse dixit* of the mandarins. Yet the need, for the health of bibliophily as a whole, of new paths and wider horizons will be pressing in any period of intense collecting activity, even without the other aggravating circumstances. For it has been the recurrent fear of collectors and commentators for the past century, and no doubt will be for the next, that the supply of books is drying up. By this of course must be understood, though it is not always understood by those who lament the loudest, the supply of books *which have been collected in the past*: and, within an area which is by now of some size, such fears have increasing substance with every passing year. It would be useless today for even a multi-millionaire to start collecting first editions of Shakespeare or the *editiones principes* of the Greek and Latin classics, with any hope of substantial achievement. Nor would he fare much better in half a dozen less spectacular fields which have yet been long and thoroughly cultivated. But we have noted, in the first part of this book, so many developments of taste

[1] See above, p. 38. [2] See p. 60.

in the past that we need have little fear for the constant expansion of bibliophilic interest in the future nor for the infinite acreage of virgin soil which is as constantly available to the pioneer. For as de Ricci said[1] in another context (whether converted by Symons or by the experience of the twenties), 'there is no conceivable subject upon which a truly enlightening collection cannot be made'.

It was no coincidence that Sadleir, Symons and de Ricci should all have stressed this particular point in the year 1930, a time, if ever there was one, for all good men to come to the aid of the party. It is within the past twenty years that the need for broadening the base of bibliophily has been, not merely perceived, but rationalised and expounded as a conscious policy by a number of collectors and booksellers. Four years later, for instance, an exhibition was held in London[2] to demonstrate by practical example the flexibility, both of subject and method of attack, inherent in a pursuit which its contemporary critics had more reason than usual for regarding as muscle-bound. In connection with this, and also under Mr Sadleir's aegis, a book was published called *New Paths in Book-Collecting*:[3] a symposium of essays in method by contributors who were about evenly divided between collectors and members of the rare book trade. And it may be noted in passing that this was only one instance of the responsible part taken in recent years by professional booksellers, not merely through their practical influence exerted in the course of business but also by their contributions to bibliophilic literature and propaganda, in the formulation and the exposition of theory, of policy and of practice in the book-collecting world. The general propagandist movement towards diversity of method, of which this book was one gambit, has certainly made some modest headway during the intervening

[1] 'Book-collecting for all purses', in *The Colophon*, part 2 (1930).

[2] On the premises of Messrs John and Edward Bumpus. Among the sections were The Expansion of an Author-Collection ('Monk' Lewis); The Evolution of 'Trade' and Publishers' Binding, 1600–1900; First Editions of War Books; The Development of the Theory of Evolution; Anglo-American First Editions; First Editions of Detective Fiction; Books printed on Coloured Paper; First Books of Private Presses; etc., etc.

[3] Edited by John Carter (Constable, 1934).

years. Yet if this is true, it is only because the general development of bibliophilic intelligence and skill has made such notable strides during the same period.

Of the many available examples of this I must content myself with the mention of two: the modern collector's attitude (*a*) to provenance, and (*b*) to presentation or association copies. Collectors have always had 'a natural tenderness for their predecessors, and a copy of a famous work is all the more regarded if its pedigree can be traced through a long series of book-loving owners'. Thus Pollard[1] a generation ago: and the feeling persists today. But the mere pleasing association of an individual copy with the name of an earlier bibliophile will nowadays be modified by some appreciation of his standards of connoisseurship. There are deliberate exceptions to this. No bibliophile can look unmoved on the small black oblong stamp of the BIBLIOTHECA HEBERIANA, however warmly he may deplore library stamps as a substitute for signatures and however mediocre may be the condition of the book in which this one is found. Nor will candidates for similar respect and affection be wanting, so long as collectors continue to deserve them: for instance, it was justly said[2] of Frank Hogan, who died in 1945, that 'if some of his books were not all that a connoisseur would have them, his bookplate marks their sojourn with a devoted and a courageous collector'.

But the laudable attention paid by collectors and the trade to the provenance of any considerable book has carried research and record beyond the sentimental into the technical area, where of recent years it has sometimes engaged a lively degree of promotional zeal. Auction houses, in particular, love to dignify a book with the note that it is 'The Black-White-Green-Brown-Grey copy'; and the inexperienced collector may be excused for supposing that a book with such a long pedigree must be of unexceptionable character and quality. The more sceptical will nowadays

[1] Loc. cit.
[2] *The Times Literary Supplement*, 15 June 1946.

appraise such a provenance in the light of the reputation for connoisseurship of each name in it. He knows that a Beckford or a Vernon book was probably a picked copy, and that if it was rebound for either, it was probably by Kalthoeber or Hering or Clark, soundly and without doctoring. He knows that those later collectors who patronised Francis Bedford were apt to get back their books washed and resized as well as bound, and he makes allowance accordingly. Experience suggests that a book from the library of C. S. Ascherson or B. B. MacGeorge, of Pickford Waller or Frank Bemis will be in unsophisticated original condition and in fine state, while a copy which satisfied C. W. Dyson Perrins, A. Edward Newton or Sir Hugh Walpole may well be neither. He remembers that 'John Drinkwater's copy, with a bibliographical note in his hand' will not necessarily be superior to H. T. Butler's copy without any note at all; that Huth and Hoe usually had fine copies but too often (for today's tastes) rebound them; that many of the Syston Park books bought by the *second* Thorold were villainously rebacked or rebound by the local binder at Grantham; that any boards-and-label volume from the Bellew Castle or Rhiwlas libraries will probably be practically 'as new'; and that, while Clement Shorter and Lord Esher admitted recased and ex-library copies, the duplicates extruded by a Parrish, a Jennings or a Sadleir in favour of better examples may quite likely be finer than those on the shelves of many very reputable collectors. He will apply, in short, every test which experience offers for discriminating, not only between modern and earlier standards of condition, but between the standards of individual collectors operating within the conventions of their time. He will distinguish between the legitimate sentiment which attaches to a book from its previous ownership by any famous collector and the guarantee of quality safely attributable to those previous owners whose connoisseurship has been approved by today's taste.

In the same way, the special attention paid during the past seventy-five years or so to inscribed or association copies has passed through an undiscriminating to a discriminating stage. The value and importance of such additions to a book as a presentation inscription, a poem or notes added in manuscript by the author, the later marks of use by some distinguished or beloved owner, will always be more purely subjective than any other factor in bibliophily. No one would dispute the superior interest over an ordinary first edition of Keats's *Poems* (1817) of a copy inscribed by Keats to Jack Robinson: no one again would dispute the superiority over Jack Robinson's copy of another presented to one of the poet's friends or even to a sufficiently eminent acquaintance: but everyone will have his own preference among the copies given to Fanny Brawne or to Shelley, to his brother George or to William Wordsworth.

Nevertheless, the ultimately subjective criteria applicable to all such associations, depending as they do on the sentiment or imagination of the individual collector, can be, and of late years have been, reduced to some sort of rough scale. Collectors have discovered by experience, for instance, that some authors were much more ready with presentation inscriptions than others; and this introduces the factor of rarity. Although inscribed copies of sixteenth- and seventeenth-century books of any kind are uncommon, there are yet exceptions: Walton loved to inscribe, his *Lives* especially, to his friends, while his contemporary Sir Thomas Browne, for example, is usually represented, if at all, in the books he gave away by the normal practice of the period—a note *ex dono authoris* in the recipient's hand. Among eighteenth-century writers, Boswell or Walpole presentations are commoner than Pope's, Pope's than Johnson's, Johnson's than Goldsmith's or even Swift's. Browning and Tennyson were much freer with inscriptions than Matthew Arnold or Walter Pater, Dickens than Thackeray, Disraeli than Bulwer Lytton, Darwin than Macaulay. Scott inscribed his poems often, his novels (for obvious reasons) very rarely: Jane Austen almost never. It is proper, therefore, that just as the rarer of two equally attractive books will be the more eagerly sought and the more highly priced, so the intrinsic interest of even the happiest association in a book should be related by the collector to its author's known habits.

The wary collector is even more firmly discriminating in his assessment of the character of the inscription itself. Unless there are extenuating circumstances, he takes a tepid view of any book after 1800 in which the connection with the author depends either on a note in the recipient's hand or on a formal 'from the author' in that of the publisher's clerk. These have veracity but hardly inspiration. He distinguishes between a copy presented by the author on publication and another inscribed, even to a friend, at a later date. More sharply still does he divide copies spontaneously presented from those which can be recognised as having been inscribed on request: though here he will sometimes wish that all authors had been as scrupulous as were, for instance, Housman, Hardy and Galsworthy, in their indication of the impersonal character of the latter.

There are many other signs of maturity in recent and contemporary bibliophily. Of the influences to which this is due something has been said in the earlier historical chapters, something more will be said shortly. Of the ways in which it expresses itself, bibliographical expertise, the study of comparative rarities and the appreciation of condition must be reserved for separate treatment. And if I return now to individuality of taste and the variety of approach involved in breaking new ground—both healthy signs of originality, enterprise and intelligence—it is for the purpose of emphasising the importance of a sense of balance in the general structure. For although I have been, and remain, a proponent of idiosyncrasy, a warm supporter of the unusual approach in book-collecting, I have detected in myself and have sometimes suspected among my book-collecting friends a tendency to a certain esotericism of taste which is analogous to, and is indeed sometimes allied with, that conscious virtuosity in technique to which I referred earlier. It is, equally with the other, a perfectly legitimate tendency in the sophisticated collector, so long as it is clearly recognised as such. But since it is the sophisticated collectors who most influence the unsophisticated, there is always a danger that their mannerisms, whether of taste or method, will be imitated (and usually exaggerated) while their underlying purpose remains unrecognised: just as many an architect who slaps on a swag here or a cupola there fondly supposes himself to be thereby qualifying for comparison with Wren or Brunelleschi.

It is amusing, it is usually instructive, it is often of genuine public interest to collect something which no one else collects, provided it is worth collecting. I doubt if anyone but Mr Thomas Balston collects the writings of John Martin or if more than three people besides myself collect the prose works of William Johnson Cory: and our lonely ploughs turn an attractive and perhaps a fruitful furrow. Again, it is a contribution to bibliophilic technique to evolve a perfectly novel method of attack upon any field of collecting, whether a new one or, perhaps more illuminating, one well cultivated already on orthodox lines. There is a real interest in a collection of books issued in serial parts, which is independent of any concern with their contents; just as a study of William Combe's literary style might be pursued, if rather expensively, without regard to the illustrator under whose name the *Tours of Doctor Syntax* are normally catalogued. Yet there is a risk, however small, that this sort of thing may lead to a rather introverted condition if it is undertaken by a beginner or as anything but a sideline even by a moderately experienced collector. The *parerga* of experts are dangerous examples, and King Charles's head has too often been found at the end of some intriguing little avenue of specialised enthusiasm. It is dull, expensive and wasteful of effort to collect what too many other people are collecting. But if the opposite extreme is always preferable, it is nevertheless also an extreme, and the *via media* is as desirable in book-collecting as elsewhere. Bibliophily in its broader aspects is a sociable and an emulative pursuit, and many a promising special line has gone sour on the collector himself because his interest could not survive the profound and persistent disinterest of his fellow-collectors. 'No man', said Donne, 'is an *Iland* intire of it self; every man is a peece of the *Continent*, a part of the *maine*.' Similarly only an eccentric can exist comfortably in a private vacuum of his own creating. And if individuality of taste is pushed too far, it becomes eccentricity, just as unconventionality of technique can degenerate into preciosity. There is room in so tolerant a community as ours for a good deal of both, as long as the main body of taste is soundly related to letters and to life, the main currents of technique to reason. But it is important for the sound development of book-collecting that a steady balance be preserved between tradition and innovation, between originality and sobriety, between radicalism and common sense.

CHAPTER VIII

THE EDUCATION OF THE COLLECTOR

No use hunting Caxtons or First Folio Shakespeares with a pop-gun.
HOLBROOK JACKSON

EVEN those who think it academic to enquire *why* people should collect and presumptuous to discuss *what*, will agree that it is sometimes useful to consider *how*. For 'mere purchasing', as Charles Monselet [1] said, 'does not constitute collecting', and those who regard ignorance as just something to wallow in are never likely to want to become book-collectors. Probably few collectors are so methodical as to put themselves through any formal education for what is, after all, a fairly sophisticated pursuit. Few, on the other hand, even of the most happy-go-lucky, have not discovered at some point in their career the advantage they have gained from some sort of informal education, and perhaps wished they had had more of it earlier. It is consequently not unprofitable for any man, on attaining that momentous, that climactic point at which he consciously recognises himself as a book-collector, to make up his mind whether his pleasure is likely to be sharpened or spoiled by some addition of technical skill. His decision will depend partly on circumstances—objectives, time, money, etc.—but more on temperament. Yet if each of us has to decide for himself how much knowledge he has the time or the inclination to acquire and how much he will cheerfully dispense with, he will first need to review the various means by which he can most satisfactorily attain his provisional target.

Foremost among these is that hard, sometimes expensive, but always invigorating method, the school of experience. There is no substitute for it: no man can learn how to collect from manuals or at second hand: and some of the happiest collectors have had no

---

[1] Quoted by Holbrook Jackson, op. cit., p. 566.

other schooling. As Winterich and Randall [1] have well said: 'The collector learns about collecting by collecting.' One of the most considerable collectors now living was showing me his books some years ago, and asking, as collectors are wont to do, what I thought of this or that copy. Since dog does not eat dog, it is sometimes difficult on these occasions for a professional to combine honesty with tact in giving an opinion of a book which the owner has bought from some other bookshop than one's own; but I remember that my comment on a brazenly doctored copy of one desirable and expensive book was distinctly lukewarm. My friend cocked an eye at me. 'Yes,' he said, 'yes, I know. It cost me a hundred thousand dollars to find out that * * * * didn't know his business.' Few collectors, fortunately, have to buy their experience so expensively. But buy it they must, whether they pay in time and effort or in money. And the earlier they learn, by trial and error and then more trial and error, the fundamentals which cannot be taught by precept, the sooner will they acquire the stability of judgment on which alone can be safely based that boldness of decision which marks the true collector. In no other field of activity is it truer that he who hesitates loses: and when collectors (or, for the matter of that, booksellers) are exchanging reminiscences, you will notice that for every book that someone regrets buying he will recall a dozen that he regrets not buying.

The school of experience holds its classes in bookshops and in the auction room. And if the auctioneer is the examiner, a good bookseller can be an invaluable tutor. It is true that in his shop, as well as at a sale, the collector pits his judgment of *price* not only against that of his fellow-collectors but also against the dealer's. In all other respects, however, and they are ultimately much more important respects, his interests and his bookseller's are one. But the bookseller's influence on book-collecting is of so special an importance that it must be reserved for separate consideration later, while we turn to those potentially educative factors in the collector's progress which are supplementary to, rather than part of, his own personal experience in buying (and of course occasionally in selling) books.

[1] *A Primer of Book-Collecting* (New York, 1946), p. 191.

Among these much the pleasantest and often the most fruitful is the exchange of ideas with other collectors, the inspection of their shelves and the comparison of experiences, whether bibliographical, technical or simply of acquisition. We have remarked earlier the lessons, both in taste and technique, which can be learnt from the study of a well-designed collection, whether described in a catalogue or making its final bow in the auction room. We have also noted a few significant examples of the effect exerted, again both on taste and technique, by the current operations of eminent collectors. These widespreading but largely impersonal influences are supplemented by the more frequent and intimate exchanges between individuals or between small groups of like-minded book-lovers, each of whom contributes his share to the common pool of experience. There are always, of course, those who prefer to play a lone hand. There are naturally some reservations between competitors in the same field. Discussion perhaps tends to retrospect rather than prospect, when it leaves the area of theory for that of practice. Yet apart from any question of its pleasure, the educative value of such interplay of ideas is inestimable. It is not only stimulating and suggestive, it is also often, and just as valuably, corrective. Lone wolves get queer ideas; and an estimate of price or rarity, a bibliographical hypothesis, or an opinion of the reliability of a particular dealer, are equally the better for being measured against the experience of others.

These advantages (self-evident, no doubt, to the point of the commonplace) were formally recognised by bibliophiles as early as 1812, with the foundation of the Roxburghe Club, the oldest and the most exclusive society of its kind in the English-speaking world. From the many other collectors' clubs, mostly founded during the past seventy-five years, it would be invidious to select examples in order of merit. But to take note of the Grolier Club of New York, the Caxton Club of Chicago, the Elizabethan Club of Yale and the Zamorano Club of Los Angeles, is instructive to English readers both as an indication of the geographical range of such societies and as a reminder that they have become as common in America as they are rare in Great Britain. The First Edition Club, for example, despite some meritorious publications, failed as a sociable nucleus: aiming at the modish, it achieved only the *chichi*. Of the Roxburghe Club itself it has been disrespectfully said that a few indubitably distinguished commoners are grudgingly admitted from time to time, as a sort of lip-service to bibliophily by a primarily patrician society. But if this is mere envy and malice, it is true that the Club plays little part in the larger book-collecting world; and its fidelity, in its publications at least, to the tastes of its founders gives it something of the air of a dinosaur— the stately but muscle-bound survivor of a vanished epoch. At the other extreme, with a membership in five figures and a seniority of less than five years, is the National Book League. And if it is too early to tell what may be the influence of its programme of anti-quarian exhibitions, it is already clear that its opportunity is being courageously grasped. This opportunity would be great in any case, since no other platform exists in London for bibliophilic propaganda: it is all the greater for the fact that while NBL's membership is by definition bookish, it is probably not more than 5 per cent book-collecting. And it will be of the greatest interest to measure the impact on substantial numbers of the literary but uninitiated public of exhibitions [1] organised and catalogued on exacting bibliophilic and bibliographical lines.

One English association of book-collectors, however, deserves a respectful if retrospective bow: namely, the Baskerville Club. Founded in Cambridge at the beginning of the present century by Charles Sayle of St John's and Mr Arthur Cole, a discriminating but unostentatious benefactor of other libraries besides that of his own college, King's, the Club's original membership included Francis Jenkinson, Maynard Keynes, Stephen Gaselee and A. T. Bartholemew. Its influence on the scholarly book-collecting habits of Cambridge was considerable; and that by 1914, when it sponsored Geoffrey Keynes's *Bibliography of Donne,* it had become of more than merely local significance is shown by the addition to the list of members of such names as W. W. Greg and Edmund Gosse.

---

[1] E.g. *Children's Books of Yesterday,* by Percy H. Muir, *Victorian Fiction,* by John Carter and Michael Sadleir, *English Poetry,* by John Hayward.

It is not an accident but a matter of national temperament that America is full and England almost empty of book-collectors' clubs. It is nevertheless ironical that what is a novelty in London should be normal and established practice in a dozen cities and universities in the United States. The Grolier Club (*primus inter pares* not in age alone) has been putting on bibliophilic exhibitions for well over half a century, many of the catalogues of which have earned a place on every self-respecting reference shelf. And the Grolier Club has many enterprising rivals. In the same way, it is not an accident but a matter of policy that the public and university libraries of America take an attitude towards rare books quite different from that which obtains in most parts of Great Britain. The show cases in the British Museum and in ULC, for example,[1] are, it is true, decently furnished with beautiful, interesting, often thrilling books, soberly but sufficiently described. Yet they too often exude an air of duty rather than of enthusiasm: and the occasional, the very occasional, special exhibitions convincingly demonstrate that their custodians would regard any sort of show-manship as being in thoroughly bad taste.

This attitude is entirely consistent with the view that an institutional library's business is to conserve and to make available to properly accredited persons the raw materials of scholarship: that it is of no concern whether a book is precious or beautiful or rare or charged with associative emotion, provided that it is simply there; and that even if staff, money and facilities were available, which of course they are not, owing to parsimony upstairs, it would still be alien to the proper function of such institutions to lure people in—whether undergraduates or the man in Great Russell Street—for a heady draught of the poetry, the imagination, the thought or the craftsmanship of the illustrious past in print.

This view of the function of a library is widely and responsibly held in the British Isles. Though I may be allowed to regret it, I do not presume to criticise it; for the integration of rare books and special collections in a great university library and their subsequent

[1] The Bodleian is slightly more enlightened. But I believe the Swift exhibition of 1945 was the first of its kind sponsored by the University Library, Cambridge, within living memory.

exploitation are no less formidable administrative problems than the function of the library itself as a living part of the university is a political one. And these are matters too wide and high for a treatise on book-collecting. Yet they affect book-collecting: and, as we have seen, book-collectors often and very significantly affect them, by their readiness or their disinclination to give, bequeath or lend to institutional libraries treasures which the latter cannot or do not care to afford. It is, therefore, within our terms of reference to compare the results of what we may call the English policy with the results of what may with equal justice (that is, rather rough justice) be called the American policy, as they affect, not scholars, students and researchers, but book-lovers and book-collectors.

Most of the major American university libraries (not to mention such public or memorial libraries as the Morgan in New York or the William Andrews Clark in Los Angeles) not only take a very lively interest in rare books *as* rare books. They also take a lively interest in collectors. And if the cynic can maintain that the latter interest sometimes has the ulterior motive of a Strasbourg goose-breeder, it is nevertheless expressed, even where this is true, with intelligence as well as solicitude. For when a university library fosters a private collection which it hopes ultimately to acquire, it is obviously even more anxious that the collecting of it should be intelligent and judicious than when its objective is the purely disinterested one of encouraging and directing a civilised and scholarly occupation among the undergraduates or graduates in the university's care. And there can be no doubt whatever that a university library whose staff can give time and attention to book-collectors (actual and potential); which provides the right atmosphere and facilities for them to absorb productive ideas and develop sensible methods, can make a very powerful and beneficial contribution to the education of book-lovers outside as well as inside the university. And it is after all the aptitudes discovered and the tastes formed in youth which bear the best fruit in maturity.

It is, for instance, unlikely (if I may select a single example without odium) that any one man has personally influenced for good more book-collectors of our time than Dr Chauncey Brewster Tinker, of Yale. Combining the Professorship of English literature with the office of Keeper of Rare Books in the Library, he has been, indeed, strategically situated to inculcate, by precept as well as example, that sense of the past by which book-collecting can humanise and enliven the study of literature. But if Dr Tinker's special capacity for inspiring a love of books (well salted, on occasion, with a certain personal intransigeance) has been, and is, his own, the atmosphere in which it is exercised is by no means peculiar to Yale. It flourishes in many other American universities; and in some it has produced what may be the beginnings of formal education in book-collecting. Pennsylvania has for a number of years had its Rosenbach Lectures, which, though dedicated (like Sandars's) to bibliography, have often strayed far into bibliophilic territory. Informal courses on various aspects of book-collecting have been held at Harvard. And a full-dress series of lectures was recently delivered at Ann Arbor by Mr Colton Storm and Mr Howard Peckham.[1]

Whether such innovations will develop remains to be seen. They are in any case impressive evidence of the disciplined enthusiasm, the enterprise and the care which American universities think well to devote to the education of collectors. And when we recall the constant stream of exhibitions, catalogues, bulletins and other bibliophilic publications which have for many years enriched the collecting scene in the United States, we cannot but feel the marked contrast in tempo, intensity and organisation between American practice and English. It would certainly be as presumptuously futile to try to impose American methods on English collectors or institutions, as to persuade the Americans to revert to our more superficially casual approach. It is doubtful how many leaves, even of those which would manifestly fit, are likely to be taken out of the American book. That some could be taken with advantage is certain. Yet there are more American critics than English of some of the present tendencies in American university library policy towards rare book-collecting.

These do not so much fear that the hot-house atmosphere, into

[1] Published as *Invitation to Book-Collecting* (New York, Bowker, 1947).

which institutional warmth occasionally degenerates, will have any serious effect on the young plants: though I myself should be apprehensive of the tendency to encourage too early and too narrow specialisation, which may produce one unrivalled collection (for the university?) but is not calculated to breed a good collector. The critics are more often perturbed by the growing preoccupation of many university libraries in the United States with rare books, as distinct from just books, both in matters of exploitation and of acquisition. Now a scholar or a student might object to this on the ground (whether well or ill founded) that the larger, long-term functions of a great working library were receiving less attention because the rare book room and the special collections were receiving more. But while it is true that it is always easier to coax a thousand dollars out of a benevolent donor for a single spectacular item than for a year's output of Russian periodicals, that aspect of the matter is not the special concern of book-collectors (or booksellers). What is their concern is the growing volume of university library buying in the rare book market, both public and private, which is the direct outcome of the greatly increased attention being paid to the rare book rooms on a hundred American campuses. Up to a point this development is obviously healthy, both as a sign of grace among dons and because competition is a good thing in itself. But whether in the long run the rare book men in the university libraries can have it both ways is another matter. Bread sown on the waters, in the shape of a liberal education in book-collecting to undergraduates, may often return in the shape of a handsome collection bequeathed by a grateful *alumnus*. The cultivation of an intelligent interest in rare books among wealthy graduates and other patrons does good in itself, as well as setting the scene for an appeal when the library wants to buy an important book for which no funds are available. The mere disinterested propagation of sound taste and technique in book-collecting is a laudable and a very proper function of a university library. But if the libraries all over a huge and wealthy continent are also going themselves to invade the auction rooms, the neglected studies of stately homes, the file sets and MS. cupboards of living writers and the various other sources normally tapped by collectors and the trade, it is conceivable that the time may come when they will drive their own pupils out of the market.

The commercial elements in book-collecting are collectors, dealers and institutional libraries (auction houses are merely a mechanical convenience). And if collectors cannot do without dealers, the rare book rooms of institutional libraries cannot do without either. Nor will they be able to until they all have ten million a year, when they could presumably do without the collectors. It is therefore questionable (so their critics argue) whether their own long-term interests are not damaged by any such tactics as might eventually convince the collectors that the game was no longer worth the candle, and put the booksellers out of business. Unless there is plenty of circulation, bibliophily cannot thrive; and the ultimate value of the bibliophile to pure scholarship as well as to the humanities of scholarship depends on his recognition as an active entity, not a mere appendix. It may be that the apprehensions of these critics are excessive, or even entirely unfounded. Yet it would perhaps do no harm if the copy of *Alice Through the Looking Glass* (1872) in the sanctum of every American university library were kept open at 'The Walrus and the Carpenter'.

No such precaution, certainly, is at present needed in England. And there are many, no doubt, who hope it never will be: who not only disapprove of university libraries concerning themselves with rare books as such, but dislike the whole idea of any conscious or concerted efforts to foster and educate collectors, believing that εὑρεῖν is better than μαθεῖν in this as well as other intellectual pursuits. These will perhaps maintain that too much polishing takes the gilt off the gingerbread, and that the enjoyment of collecting is impaired by too strict an attention to technique. They will probably introduce the comparison between 'professionals' and 'amateurs', with the native English preference for the latter and a blithe disregard for the connotation of the word among Continental bibliophiles. They believe, in short, that book-collectors should be left to their own devices and should neither be taken too seriously themselves nor encouraged to take their collecting too seriously.

It is not, fortunately, my duty to express an opinion on the merits of these opposing points of view. I think it possible that American developments have been rather more rapid and rather more intensive than may be entirely healthy in a pursuit whose practitioners are happiest when the nice balance between the imagination and the intellect, between careless rapture and scientific rigour, is neither endangered nor even too precisely defined. On the other hand, there is no denying that many English collectors would benefit, especially in youth, from a rather warmer shoulder from academic and official bodies and persons than they commonly encounter.[1] And if it is considered hazardous to press education on potentially carefree book-collectors or to bring too much calculation to their encouragement, yet it is possibly not wholly due to this high principle that so little of either is made available in England to those of them, however few they may be, who would welcome and profit by both if they were to be had for the asking.

[1] The Bibliographical Society is an honourable exception to this generalisation.

CHAPTER IX

TOOLS AND TERMINOLOGY

Around the bibliographer's table there lies a passionless calm, unruffled
by politics or sex-problems.   NORMAN DOUGLAS

'THE two principal aids to the formation of a library', says
Hazlitt,[1] with all the solemnity of capitals, 'are Personal
Observation and Works of Reference.' In the previous
chapter we considered various supplementary and optional factors
in the collector's education, after recognising the paramount importance of Hazlitt's first principle; and we must now consider his
second. For even the collector who prefers to play an entirely
solitary hand, or another who is determined not to complicate his
simple pleasures with abstruse bibliographical technicalities, is
nevertheless inevitably dependent to some extent on reference
books. He may abjure the slide-rule for the clasp-knife, but he
cannot work altogether without tools.

Some collectors take readily to bibliography and the minutiae of
technique. Others are early convinced that their enjoyment will be
spoiled thereby; and some of these not only continue to profess,
but succeed in genuinely maintaining, a sturdy indifference to the
most seductive niceties of priority, the subtlest attractions of an
issue point. (In the same way, one has known people who persist
in flaunting that metaphorical straw between the teeth after years
of urban residence.) But most collectors take bibliography as it
comes: acquiring what they need as their collections develop,
educating themselves *ad hoc* rather than on any conscious plan, and
only troubling to learn how a sheet is made up in duodecimo when
they are brought up against it by some specific problem. On their
first encounters with what are commonly called 'points', these
reasonable creatures will be fascinated or repelled according to their
individual temperaments. But even he who decides that many of
them are much ado about nothing must base his decision on some

[1] Op. cit., p. 260.

acquaintance with the bibliographical principles on which 'points' depend, if he is to distinguish between the substantial and the trivial, the genuine and the factitious examples. Any mule can be obstinate. To be strong-minded requires not only strength of character but also the use of the mind.

In practice, the collector will be brought up against the whole question of points, issues and the like at a very early stage, for in these days booksellers' catalogues are freely studded with them and it is unlikely that his own particular quarry will be any more immune from such complications than another. Moreover, tricky books stand out in any list, whether an author-bibliography or a dealer's catalogue, simply by virtue of their trickiness. For, as Mr Curle[1] has observed, 'once a bibliographical point gets recognised, it achieves, whether right or wrong, whether important or unimportant, that kind of notoriety which the unusual always invites. Books without points are like women without beauty— they pass unnoticed in the crowd. But books with points excite immediate interest and everybody, so to speak, turns to gaze at them. And therefore there is an instinctive tendency to dwell on points, to exaggerate their significance, and even to discover points that are not really points at all.' It is the recognition of this instinct, in others, if not in themselves, that causes many a commonsensical collector to adopt a hard-boiled, negative attitude to all points, to consider them (if I may borrow Mr Curle's simile) not beauty-spots but warts. The discriminating collector will hardly be content with this impatient solution: he will accept the implied injunction to be cautious, but he will want his caution well founded.

The connotation of the magic word 'point' is pretty well understood by collectors, and I need do no more here than give a few examples[2] of the genuine and the bogus variety.

[1] Op. cit., p. 85.
[2] Several of these are drawn from Percy H. Muir's two volumes, *Points* and *Points: Second Series*, which contain much excellent sense on their subject, pungently expressed.

(1) *Title-page variations*

The changed address in the publishers' imprint in Lamb's *Essays of Elia* (1823) and Mrs Browning's *Poems* (second edition, 2 vols., 1850) is significant, for Waterloo Place and Piccadilly respectively represent moves made by their publishers after the original title-pages were printed. But variant title-pages in seventeenth- and eighteenth-century books—e.g. the *Second Folio* of Shakespeare (1632) or Herbert's *The Temple* (1633), Locke's *An Essay concerning Humane Understanding* (1690) or Lamb's *A Tale of Rosamond Gray* (1798)—where several distributors shared the edition, need not *necessarily* be other than simultaneous in issue. As for that often-quoted 'point', the misprinted date MDCLXXI for MDCCLXXI on the title-page of *Humphrey Clinker*, it is so far from significant that it occurs in both the first edition and the undifferentiated (but quite distinct) reprint.

(2) *Textual changes*

Cancels, as exemplified in such books as Boswell's *Johnson* (2 vols., 1791)—e.g. the passage on conjugal infidelity; Beckford's *Thoughts on Hunting* (Salisbury, 1781)—e.g. the passage on bloodlust among sportsmen; and Scott's *Marmion* (1808)—e.g. the lines added to the panegyric on Charles James Fox; or even the substitution of 'with the aid of the illustrations' for 'with the aid of the illustrious Leech' in the preface to *Handley Cross* (first illustrated edition, 1854)—these are significant, because they represent purposeful textual alterations made after the books were completely printed off: even if, as in the first three cases, these changes were made before publication, so that the result is two 'states' and not two 'issues'.

The corrections by cancel of the misprinted 'Misellaneous' in the contents page of Shelley's *Prometheus Unbound* (1820) or of the misdated title-page of Conrad's *Chance* (1913) have no interest of text: but both make a proper bibliographical 'point'. The transposed lines found on p. 335 of some copies of *South Wind* (1917), on the other hand, are neither interesting nor significant, for it has been established that the types were correctly in place when printing started, came loose during the run and were replaced out of order. Nor is the absence of punctuation in the first two lines on p. 52 of Housman's *Last Poems* (1922) a sign of 'first issue', as it is often stated to be; for the error was constant during the entire run.

(3) *Illustrations*

A re-engraved or altered plate, such as the first ('The Royal Academy') in Ackermann's *Microcosm of London* (3 vols., 1808–10), often makes a valid issue point. Signs of progressive wear or of rebitten passages in an unaltered plate can, when unmistakably established, provide evidence of early or late printing. But many of the variations in the plates of Dickens's novels from *Nicholas Nickleby* (1839) to *David Copperfield* (1850) have no bearing on the priority of one copy over another, for the steels were prepared and printed off in duplicate (or more) before gathering started.

(4) *Advertisements*

In general, advertisements which are part of the collation are usually significant, while for those which are inserted significance needs to be definitely established. The three distinct issues of Maugham's *The Moon and Sixpence* (1919) depend entirely on the advertisements for their identification: in *Of Human Bondage* (1915), on the other hand, the presence or absence of a publisher's catalogue is quite immaterial. And whereas *Robinson Crusoe* (1719) is positively incomplete without its advertisement leaves, since they are part of the last signature, it was a matter of pure chance whether *The Confessions of an English Opium Eater* (1822) was boarded up with one, two, four or eight leaves, or none at all.

(5) *Completeness*

Gibbon's *Miscellaneous Works* are normally counted as complete in two volumes, 1796, though a third, also in quarto, was issued in 1815. It is perhaps equally permissible to say that John Dalton's *A New System of Chemistry* was issued in two volumes (Manchester, 1808, 1810), on the ground that the third, supplementary, volume did not appear until 1827. It is debatable whether *Wuthering*

Heights (1847), complete in its two volumes, is a real entity without *Agnes Grey*, which formed the third volume of that unconventionally conventional three-decker. The errata leaves which are found in some copies of Copernicus's *De Revolutionibus Orbium Coelestium* (Nuremberg, 1543) and Browne's *Urne Buriall and the Garden of Cyrus* (1658) were probably not issued with the earliest copies; so that if their presence justifies the description 'complete with the errata leaf', their absence equally allows 'early issue before the printing of the errata leaf'. But supplements or 'additions and corrections' such as are occasionally bound up with Blackstone's *Commentaries on the Laws of England* (4 vols., Oxford, 1765–8) and Chesterfield's *Letters* (2 vols., 1774) are not part of the book; and the plates of the *Founders* are no more integral to Ackermann's *Oxford* (2 vols., 1814) because they are often bound in, than the apology sheet which is occasionally found inserted in it is part of *A Sentimental Journey* (2 vols., 1768).

Half-titles are of course a necessity where they are called for, though in a few cases, such as Pope's *Essay on Criticism* (1711) and Gray's *Poems* (1768), the first volume of *The Last Days of Pompeii* (3 vols., 1834) and the last of Disraeli's *Sybil* (3 vols., 1845), they have sometimes been called for unnecessarily. In others, such as Sheridan's *The Critic* (1781), the absence of the half-title is so overwhelmingly frequent that some have been tempted (without justification, in my view) to suppose that part of the edition was issued without it.

Blank leaves offer a problem of their own. When they are part of the signature, their presence is strictly necessary to the completeness of the book: and if it is customary (and reasonable) to treat with some indulgence their absence from a rare incunable or *STC* period volume, standards become increasingly rigorous with the decreasing antiquity and rarity of the book. But collectors of American first editions of the mid-nineteenth century have noted that the presence and number of blank leaves at the beginning and end of many cloth-bound books of that period are so widely variable as to make certainty of collation almost impossible.

(6) *Bindings*

Many 'points' of authentic significance have been established among the innumerable binding variants found on nineteenth- and twentieth-century books issued in cloth (variant styles of paper-backed boards are seldom significant). From the geometric design on the Aylott and Jones issue of the Brontës' *Poems* (1846) and the price '4/6' on the spine of *The Golden Treasury* (Cambridge, 1861) to *Green Mansions* (1904) without the publisher's design on the back cover, first editions bound up in successive batches have all too frequently developed subdivisions of issue amongst which priority can only sometimes be determined. If the status of the variant bindings on Browning's *Men and Women* (2 vols., 1855) and Somerville and Ross's *The Real Charlotte* (3 vols., 1894) is pretty well established, the utmost caution must hedge any conclusion as to the priority between the first four of the five bindings on George Eliot's *Felix Holt* (3 vols., 1866), between any but perhaps the first of the ten so far recorded for Meredith's *The Shaving of Shagpat* (1856) and even between the three variants of what is almost certainly the earliest of the three bindings on Hardy's *A Pair of Blue Eyes* (3 vols., 1873). As for the variations in the cloth cases of Dickens's part-issued novels, they are so numerous and baffling that no one has yet attempted even to describe, let alone classify them.

In conclusion, it must be noted that English fiction between 1830 and the late fifties was frequently issued alternatively in full cloth gilt and in half cloth with paper labels. The myth that the latter style is *ipso facto* either inferior or later is now current only in the backwoods.

The printed matter on which the collector can draw for his own education is of an immense variety of subject and a very considerable variety of approach. It ranges from the elementary primer, such as Muir's *Book-Collecting as a Hobby*,[1] to specialised studies like Hobson's *Maioli, Canevari and others*[2] or the Pottles' index to

[1] Gramol Publications, 1945.   [2] Ernest Benn, 1926.

the Boswell papers.[1] Among the manuals, guide-books and discursive reminiscences of collectors, the available books are designed for, or unconsciously appeal to, collectors in varying stages of development. Some, like A. Edward Newton's several beguiling books,[2] are infectious to the general reader as well as to the professed collector. Other, like Iolo Williams's *Elements of Book-Collecting*[3] or Winterich and Randall's *A Primer of Book-Collecting*[4] or Storm and Peckham's *Invitation to Book-Collecting*,[5] while modestly addressing themselves to the beginner, have also had the more experienced practitioners as clearly in mind as did their predecessors Thomas Frognall Dibdin, John Hill Burton, J. H. Slater, W. Carew Hazlitt or Seymour de Ricci, whose observations have been quoted here and there in the present work. There is, it is true, a dearth of advanced treatises of a general kind, specifically aimed at the graduate collector: and for very obvious reasons. It requires a temerity of which no one can be more conscious than one who is now attempting it, to philosophise at the feet of a whole circle of Gamaliels.

Much of the advanced reading in general bibliophily is in fact to be found among the various periodicals. Of these *The Book-Collector's Quarterly* (1930-7) and *The Colophon* (1930-40, now revived as *The New Colophon*) were primarily devoted to collecting, with pure bibliography in secondary place. Yet specifically bibliographical periodicals have not ignored collectors. And a good deal of applied, as well as pure, science may be found in the transactions of the Bibliographical Societies of London,[6] New York,[7] Oxford and Edinburgh, and in the bulletins or quarterlies of such libraries as Bodley, Huntington, Harvard, the New York Public, or Boston. Few collectors, indeed, can get far in their bibliographical education without reference if not subscription to some at least of these; for it is as true of bibliographers as of classical

[1] F. A. and M. S. Pottle, *The Private Papers of James Boswell from Malahide Castle, etc. A Catalogue* (Oxford University Press, 1931).
[2] E.g. *The Amenities of Book-Collecting* (Boston, 1918).
[3] Elkin Mathews and Marrot, 1924.
[4] New York, Greenberg, 1946.   [5] New York, Bowker, 1947.
[6] *The Library*, published quarterly by the Oxford University Press.
[7] *The Papers of the Bibliographical Society of America*, quarterly.

scholars that their most brilliant *adversaria* often fail to get collected into book form. It is a melancholy commonplace that collectors and the trade have been halting in support of specifically bibliophilic periodicals, whose lives have almost always been precarious and all too often brief. And it is sad that one strictly bibliographical periodical designed entirely for, and dependent on contributions from, the collecting world should have gone the same way: namely, the late lamented *Bibliographical Notes and Queries*.[1]

There are also the annual summaries of auction records, English[2] and American,[3] to which the alert collector must often refer, even if he does not possess them. These contribute to practical rather than theoretical education, for they are almost as little concerned with bibliography as the learned quarterlies are with prices. We shall consider later the relation between auction prices and book-shop prices, and these annuals are mentioned among bibliophilic literature mainly for a word of warning. Hazlitt[4] was perhaps over-severe when he described those[5] current in his day as 'little better than mechanical transcripts from the auctioneers' extremely treacherous catalogues, [made] by outsiders'. The auctioneers' catalogues are today certainly less 'treacherous'; but although *American Book-Prices Current* is edited with scrupulous care, the English annuals leave much to be desired. It is unfortunately still true to say, with Hazlitt,[6] that they 'cannot be trusted as an authority or a guide by any person who does not approach them with a certain measure of experience', to which I would add that if experience is lacking, scepticism may be substituted.

But if the collector has made his preliminary reconnaissance among the manuals, and if he maintains his regular patrols among the periodicals, the main body of bibliographical literature is to be found in the reference books, the catalogues of great collections,

[1] Elkin Mathews Ltd., London, and Scribners, New York, 1935–9.
[2] *Book-Auction Records*, quarterly parts and annual volumes, Henry Stevens Son and Stiles: *Book-Prices Current*, annual volumes, Witherby.
[3] *American Book-Prices Current*, annual, New York, Bowker.
[4] Op. cit., p. 262.   [5] *BAR, BPC* and *Book Sales*.
[6] Op. cit., p. 263.

author-bibliographies, studies of special periods or categories, and finally in certain technical treatises, one or another of which may be relevant to his particular field. To his attack on any substantial part of this material an almost indispensable preliminary is some study of McKerrow's *Introduction to Bibliography*,[1] that classic exposition of general principles which immediately became and is likely to remain the standard work on its subject.[2] It is perhaps not strictly necessary to have mastered more than the rudiments of collation, book-structure and publishing practice to find one's way about Lowndes[3] or Merle Johnson,[4] Allibone[5] or Halkett and Laing,[6] Brunet[7] or Hain,[8] to name a handful of the basic 'omnibus' reference books. But others of the same category can hardly be understood, let alone used with profit, by the innocent; and among such would be found many besides *STC*,[9] the *Gesamtkatalog der Wiegendrucke*[10] and Sabin and Eames's massive *Bibliotheca Americana*.[11]

Important, indeed in many cases crucial extension, supplement and amplification to the information extricable from the great basic reference books is provided by the annotated catalogues of private libraries and of special exhibitions organised by universities or bibliophile societies. Among the latter, the publications of the Grolier Club have already been mentioned, while the particulars of the numerous catalogues of centenary exhibitions and the like are readily found under their authors in any major library. Among the former, collectors of English literature are particularly indebted

---

[1] Oxford University Press, 1927.

[2] Those who quail before McKerrow's admittedly formidable array of technicalities can secure a pass degree with Arundell Esdaile's excellent and rather less exacting *A Student's Manual of Bibliography* (Allen and Unwin, 1931).

[3] See above, p. 32.

[4] *American First Editions* (1928; fourth edition, revised by Jacob Blanck, New York, Bowker, 1942).

[5] *Critical Dictionary of English Literature.*

[6] *Dictionary of Anonymous and Pseudonymous English Literature* (latest edition, Edinburgh, 1926–34).

[7] *Manuel du Libraire et de l'Amateur de Livres* (Paris, 1842–4).

[8] *Repertorium Bibliographicum* (Stuttgart, 1826–38), and a facsimile reprint.

[9] *Short Title Catalogue of English Books printed before* 1640 (The Bibliographical Society, 1926; reprint 1946). [10] Leipzig, still in progress.

[11] New York, Bibliographical Society of America, 29 vols., 1868–1936.

to the Huth[1] and Church catalogues, the several Widener catalogues, the Ashley catalogue, the Dormy House series,[2] the Pforzheimer catalogue, and a dozen more similarly wide-ranging assemblages, fully and informatively described. Specialists are often able to rely on such comprehensive works in their kind as Darlow and Moule's great catalogue of Bibles, or the Schwerdt catalogue of *Hunting, Hawkings and Shooting*; Mr George Arents's tobacco collection or M. André Simon's *Bibliotheca Bacchica*; the Osler catalogue of medical or the Wheeler Gift catalogue of scientific literature. Similar assistance in the field of early printed and early illustrated books is provided by the J. P. Morgan, Fairfax Murray and other catalogues, of bindings by those of Hoe, Mortimer Schiff or Mme Whitney-Hoff; and the list could easily be extended for a couple of pages without descending to secondary sources.

Next come the bibliographical treatments, whether enumerative or descriptive, of a class of literature, a period or a subject. Examples of the first are Greg's monumental *Bibliography of the English Printed Drama to the Restoration*,[3] Arundell Esdaile's *English Tales and Prose Romances before* 1740[4] or John Hayward's catalogue of *English Poetry*.[5] Typical of the second would be Iolo Williams's *Points in Eighteenth-Century Verse*,[6] Sadleir's *Excursions in Victorian Bibliography*[7] or Danielson's *Bibliographies of Modern Authors*.[8] The bibliographical studies of subjects are more difficult to classify, since many of them deal with highly specialised fields. But some indication of this elastic species may be given by such examples as Schreiber's *Manuel de l'Amateur de la Gravure sur Bois*,[9]

---

[1] Most of the catalogues referred to in this paragraph were privately printed, so that details would be academic.

[2] Parrish always studiously disclaimed the bibliographer's approach. But except for shortcomings in formal collation, he faithfully described the evidence before him, as a basis for the judgment of others, so that his chosen Victorians are in fact bibliographically very well served.

[3] Bibliographical Society, vol. 1, 1939; vol. 2 to come.

[4] Bibliographical Society, 1912.

[5] National Book League, 1947.

[6] Constable, 1934 (Bibliographia Series, No. 7).

[7] Chaundy and Cox, 1922.   [8] *The Bookman's Journal*, 1921.

[9] Berlin, 5 vols., 1891–1910.

Allen T. Hazen's *A Bibliography of the Strawberry Hill Press*,[1] Straus and Dent's *John Baskerville*,[2] Miss Blakey's *The Minerva Press*,[3] Stanley Morison's *The English Newspaper*,[4] Howard C. Levis's *Bibliography of Books in English relating to Engraving*,[5] Forrest Reid's *Illustrators of the Sixties*,[6] Turner Berry and Johnson's *Catalogue of Specimens of Printing Types*,[7] or Choulant's *History and Bibliography of Anatomic Illustration*.[8]

Often closely allied to these and often equally important to the collector whose field they touch, are a whole range of technical studies concerned more with the background of bibliography than with bibliography itself. And here again we must content ourselves with a few characteristic samples. If A. W. Pollard's *Shakespeare's Fight with the Pirates*[9] is specialised in date and Professor Percy Simpson's *Proof-Reading*[10] in scope, both teach useful lessons far beyond their immediate subjects. Neither collectors of autographs nor of inscribed copies can afford to be unacquainted with such treatises as Osborn's *Questioned Documents*[11] or R. B. Haselden's *Scientific Aids for the Study of Manuscripts*.[12] The collector of printing will of course rely on Updike's *Printing types, their History, Forms and Use*[13], but he does not forget that Proctor[14] and Dr Scholderer[15] have much to teach him about greek types, Mr Morison about the chancery italics[16] and 'Paul Beaujon' about Garamond.[16] The collector of bindings needs access to Olivier:[17] but G. D. Hobson's books[18] require reading, whether owned or borrowed; and if he

---

[1] Yale University Press, 1942.   [2] Chatto and Windus, 1907.
[3] Bibliographical Society, 1939.   [4] Cambridge University Press, 1932.
[5] Ellis, 1912.   [6] Faber and Gwyer, 1928.
[7] Oxford University Press, 1935.
[8] Translated by Mortimer Frank, University of Chicago Press, 1920.
[9] Cambridge University Press, 1920.   [10] Oxford University Press, 1935.
[11] Albany, Boyd Printing Co., 2nd ed., 1929.
[12] Bibliographical Society, 1935.
[13] Harvard University Press, 2nd ed., 1937.
[14] E.g. *The Printing of Greek in the Fifteenth Century* (Bibliographical Society, 1900).
[15] E.g. *Greek Printing Types*, 1465–1927 (British Museum, 1927).
[16] In *The Fleuron* and elsewhere.
[17] Eugène Olivier and others, *Manuel de l'Amateur de Reliures Armoriées Françaises*, 30 vols., Paris, 1924–31.
[18] E.g. *Reliures à la Fanfare*, 1935; *Bindings in Cambridge Libraries*, 1929.

omitted to buy Mr E. P. Goldschmidt's *Gothic and Renaissance Bookbindings*[1] when (shame on the publisher) he could have had it at a remainder price, he must pay a higher now if he wants the standard book in its field. The collector of eighteenth-century books will neglect Dr Chapman's treatise on *Cancels*[2] at his peril, just as the collectors of yellow-backs or music first editions or serial issues will hardly ignore the essays on those subjects by Mr Sadleir, Mr C. B. Oldman and Mr Graham Pollard in *New Paths in Book-Collecting*.[3]

The last main category of reference literature is probably the most familiar to the average collector. For author-bibliographies are more quoted by booksellers than almost any other books. It would be the most invidious category from which to select examples, if such were needed: for fortunately they are not, since the nature of an author-bibliography is self-evident. A number have been mentioned in the course of the present work; and since I have throughout chosen to cite as examples of anything only such books as I respect, it may be taken that these, though of course by no means only these, are exempt from the *caveat* which it is certainly necessary to enter against the happy confidence commonly reposed by beginners (and by some who should know better) in any bibliography of any author simply because it has got itself into print. For we have marked, however briefly, the development of the author-bibliography as a unit in the evolution of collecting technique, and we must recall that it is barely three quarters of a century old. During this period perhaps a score of really first-class performances have been achieved, and perhaps as many respectable ones. But if that combined number be subtracted from the total of author-bibliographies which profess to be more than handlists—which conform more or less, that is to say, to the ample formula originally evolved by Buxton Forman and Wise—we shall find a formidable number to which one user at least would deny more than a quite modest degree of merit. And it is of importance to any collector who is, or is likely to be,

[1] Benn, 1928.   [2] Constable, 1930 (Bibliographia Series, No. 3).
[3] Constable, 1934.

practically interested in an author of whose works a full-dress bibliography exists, to be able to estimate its reliability in advance, rather than following it blindly until he is tripped up.

It is not too much to say that no bibliography, however scholarly in conception and however meticulous in execution, is either complete or free from error. It is true, at the other end of the scale, that even the most imperfect bibliography will probably have something to teach even a veteran collector of the author concerned. But if the latter learns to cultivate humility, the less experienced will endeavour to fashion some sort of yardstick with which to measure the pretensions of his would-be guide. It is not difficult to detect brazen incompetence, even when it does not approach that of a recent authority who described signatures as 'numbers continuing at odd intervals throughout the book'. Nor is the touch of mastery easily mistaken, even when it is exercised on material with which one is unfamiliar. The more frequent and more taxing problem is presented by the large body of painstaking work which falls between the two extremes. Here accuracy of the matter presented can of course only be assessed by comparing the collations and descriptions with copies of the books themselves: and half a dozen samples will usually suffice. But the bibliographer's handling of his matter and his presentation of evidence for a conclusion will often demonstrate his quality even more promptly. 'Accuracy', said Housman [1] once, 'is a duty and not a virtue.' And this is as true of bibliography as of textual criticism, for a faulty collation is less obvious and therefore more persistently harmful than a fallacious deduction or a suspiciously dogmatic assertion, either of which carries its own red light for the critical reader. Yet there is more to bibliography than mere accuracy. As Housman put it on another [2] occasion: 'Knowledge is good, method is good, but one thing beyond all others is necessary; and that is to have a head, not a pumpkin, on your shoulders, and brains, not pudding, in your head.'

[1] Preface to *Manilius*, Book v (1930).
[2] 'The Application of Thought to Textual Criticism' in the *Proceedings of the Classical Association*, vol. XVIII (1922), p. 84.

The author-bibliography has its pendants, in the shape of bibliographical analyses of individual books—Dr Greg on the First
Quarto of *King Lear*,[1] Dr Willoughby on the printing of the First
Folio,[2] Mr James Pershing on *Paradise Lost*,[3] Mr Harold Williams
on *Gulliver's Travels*[4] or Mr Jacob Blanck on Irving's *Salmagundi*,[5]
to name a few at randon. And if, as a category, it shares with the
basic general reference books a strong claim on the attention of the
average collector, an equivalent attention is (appropriately and not
at all accidentally) paid to both in that department of reading
matter which is a staple for all collectors and the only bibliographical stamping-ground of many—the booksellers' catalogues.
The amount of bibliographical information which is subjoined to
the bare description of a book and the mention of its price varies
widely in different catalogues, but in the more careful it has increased considerably on both sides of the Atlantic during the past
twenty-five years. For the practice of the trade, and in America
also of the auctioneers, has followed—indeed has now and again
paced—the general increase in bibliographical appetite among collectors. There have always been, and no doubt there always will be,
conservative booksellers who regard all bibliographers as a nuisance
and all 'points' as pieces of finicking nonsense maliciously invented
to reduce the value of books on their own shelves. These yearn for
the good old days when no one either knew or cared about half-
titles or original cloth and they will admit, when pressed, to the
belief that the less collectors know, the better.

At the other end of the scale are those cynical characters who
regard bibliographical details as just so much attractive packaging
for their wares. If they cannot buy the stuff by the yard, they
at least care little whether the pieces fit or whence they come.
Anyone in print is an authority if what he says suits their book,
but they would turn a blind eye to Pollard or Wilberforce Eames
himself if the reverse were the case. Of this type of cataloguer
Mr Curle[6] has said: 'I fear that his optimism often outruns his

[1] Bibliographical Society, 1939.　　[2] Bibliographical Society, 1932.
[3] In *The Library*, vol. XXII, no. 1 (1941).
[4] In *The Library*, vol. VI, no. 3 (1925).
[5] In *The Papers of the Bibliographical Society of America*, vol. XVI, no. 1 (1947).
[6] Op. cit., p. 88.

knowledge and that hope, rather than necessity, is at times the mother of his invention.' This is the charitable verdict of a collector: but the matter was once put more brutally by a member of the trade.[1] 'A bookseller [he wrote] who manufactures a freak point, a bookseller who quotes a professional issue-monger whom he does not himself trust, a bookseller who, either by *suggestio falsi* or *suppressio veri*, contrives to distort bibliography for profit—all these are prostituting something which does not belong to them, and, what is more, discrediting something whose value to them depends on its scrupulous integrity.'

These, however, are the extremes. The collector will quickly learn to be wary of both the genuine (but, to him, sometimes dangerous) indifference of the shell-backs and the perverted ingenuity of the cynics. If the latter were not provided with inept bibliographies to quote from, their temptations would be less, and the sooner the collector begins to distinguish between the reliable and the unreliable bibliographers, the more readily will he distrust any bookseller who openly flouts that distinction. Yet in justice to those who regard minutiae as inventions of the devil, if not of the bibliographer, it must be allowed that there have been cases where a really thorough bibliography of a tolerably complicated author has apparently stifled rather than stimulated his collectors. Where the conscientious bibliographer reveals uncertainty, as Mr Macdonald over *Absalom and Achitophel*, Part 2 (1682), or where the doctors disagree, as over *Paradise Lost* (1667), *The Dunciad* (1728), *Candide* (? Paris, 1759) and *Faust* (Leipzig, 1790), it is natural enough that both collectors and booksellers sometimes fight a little shy of the book. The same result follows, though less markedly, where a substantial body of informed opinion dissents from the established verdict, as over the priority between the two unauthorised editions (1642) of *Religio Medici*. It was not, however, any uncertainty but, on the contrary, the appalling clarity with which the innumerable minor variants in the Waverley novels were exposed by Greville Worthington,[2] the innumerable states and issues of text, plates and advertisements in the Dickens part-

---

[1] *Publisher's Weekly*, 19 November 1932, p. 1924.
[2] *Bibliography of the Waverley Novels* (Bibliographia Series, no. 4, 1931).

issues tabulated by Hatton and Cleaver,[1] that caused many keen collectors of both either to stop collecting or at best to despair of achieving even approximate correctness and therefore to resign themselves to lowered standards.

Yet it is not among the extremists, but among the ordinary rank and file of reputable and more or less knowledgeable booksellers that the collectors will mostly move. And in their catalogues he will find not only much pertinent and valuable information but also a fair amount of bibliographical comment, deduction and occasionally hypothesis on which to exercise his judgment. I cannot wholly agree with Mr Goldschmidt[2] that 'it is the privilege of the bookseller to advance a bold hypothesis that will enhance the interest of his books as long as it is plausible. Not on him, but on the coolly sceptical historian rests the duty to demolish what cannot be strictly demonstrated'. This would be all very well if all booksellers were as learned and responsible as Mr Goldschmidt himself: but they are not, and it would be an invitation to abuse by the least, rather than the most, responsible among them if such a principle were generally accepted. Yet a number of bibliographical discoveries are in fact announced, and a much greater number of bibliographical theories are aired, in booksellers' catalogues every year; and even the collector who has most determinedly decided not to get involved in bibliography is consequently liable to be involved in it, whether he likes it or not, every time he sits down to the catalogue of any one of the fifty or so most considerable dealers in England and America.

Nor is it simply that he is thus constantly exposed to information. He cannot even read a catalogue intelligently unless he knows what the cataloguer is talking about. Moreover, even if cataloguers do all talk approximately the same language, they speak it with widely varying inflections and connotations, so that the collector finds himself compelled to exercise his own bibliographical judgment at every turn. No longer could Hazlitt[3] observe easily that 'of what he reads in the catalogues he may

[1] *Bibliography of the Periodical Works of Charles Dickens* (Chapman and Hall, 1933).
[2] *Studies in Retrospect* (The Bibliographical Society, 1945), p. 178.
[3] Op. cit., p. 261.

believe as much or as little as he likes'; for catalogues since Hazlitt's day have increased greatly in elaboration, and liking must give way to necessity. The imposing array of bibliographical support for an entry and the detailed description of a book's condition, which are now the norm for items of any importance, have brought with them, unfortunately but perhaps inevitably, a great confusion in the terminology used by cataloguers.

This confusion is of three kinds. There is, first, uncertainty in a good many matters of purely bibliographical description; there are, secondly, differences of policy and practice; and thirdly there is a wide discrepancy in standards of connoisseurship. For the first of these confusions the collector should blame, for the most part, not the booksellers but the bibliographers. If the experts cannot agree, as they cannot, on certain points fundamental to the description of whole categories of books, it is no wonder that workaday tradesmen take either the line of least resistance or the line of most attraction. 'First edition, first issue', for example, has a comfortable, reassuring sound. Often enough it is accurately used, with a connotation of fairly wide acceptance. But it will continue to be used in a number of contexts where it is at least of doubtful application until—indeed probably long after—some supreme court of bibliography lays down once and for all a precise definition of the related terms 'edition', 'impression', 'issue', 'state' and 'variant' (on the last of which most of us have fallen back at one time or another in despair of general agreement on the meaning of its two predecessors). McKerrow's rulings in this thorny matter are not entirely satisfactory either for all dates or all bibliophilic needs: yet it might be well if they were firmly adopted, even at the expense of some injustice, until something better has been evolved by an equivalent authority. It must not be thought that I am under any illusions as to the difficulties which will face the supreme court in this particular matter. And if any one else is disposed to underrate them, let him apply McKerrow's or any other system to the description of the last four or five editions of the *Encyclopaedia Britannica*, and see how far he can get without contracting brain fever.

A less hackneyed example of uncertainty, but one which causes frequent trouble, is the degree to which the sheet should be considered as a valid unit for claiming priority between one copy and another. As more and more books of the seventeenth and eighteenth century are subjected to really rigorous examination, it is being recognised first that few copies of the same edition are quite identical and secondly that only the merest chance will have brought together at the folding-bench a series of gatherings showing the earliest state of all twelve (shall we say) passages at which alterations were made in the text during printing. By the Procrustean standards of earlier days only such a copy would have qualified as 'first issue', and other copies would now and again be 'made up' to conform to an artificial optimum. Today, though we accept the bibliographical evidence [1] for a more rational view of these permutations, we have not yet evolved any acceptable, let alone generally accepted, method of classifying the results. The distinction between reprinting of sheets and alterations made during the run has been established after intensive research, for some books, such as *Robinson Crusoe*, *Gulliver's Travels* and *Tom Jones*. In a multitude of others, of which *The Vicar of Wakefield* and *The Good Natur'd Man* are notorious examples, it remains obscure. And even where the distinction is clear, the collector's estimation of the result continues uncertain.

[1] The matter was summed up as long ago as 1906 in Pollard and Greg's classic paper, *Some Points in Bibliographical Description* (reprinted separately in 1909, from the *Transactions of the Bibliographical Society*). After expounding the reasons for these minor variations, the authors continue: 'The important thing to bear in mind with regard to these differences is that if they are at all frequent in a particular work, no two copies probably will be found to agree throughout, nor will any one copy exhibit consistently earlier readings than any other copy. In the case of alterations which were made deliberately, the late pulls will tend to be more correct than the earlier, while in those due to the displacement of types, the earlier will tend to be more correct than the later. Since, however, the sheets of a book after being dried were usually gathered indiscriminately, a first-stage reading in sheet A may be found in the same copy as a last-stage reading in sheet B. Thus to speak, as has sometimes been the case, as if these alterations constituted distinct stages, and to say, for instance, that a volume belongs to an early or late issue (on analogy with the states of an etching or engraving) is wholly misleading.'

In the matter of differences of policy and practice, the bookseller must again be absolved of a large share of the blame for the oddities which sometimes disfigure his catalogues. And here the culprit is not so often the bibliographer as the collector. If one bookseller attaches more, and another less, importance to large paper impressions, proof copies, advance copies, first separate editions, off-prints and the like, it is because collectors differ so widely in their estimates, not merely of the interest of these things but also of their status—a point on which the bibliographers are for the most part perfectly clear and explicit. Again, collectors have never really made up their collective mind about serials, which constitute the first printing of many works highly prized in book form, particularly novels, and often show interesting differences of text into the bargain. Most collectors are aware of this: yet complete sets of the serialisation of *Trilby* [1] or *Tess of the D'Urbervilles*, [2] to select a pair of examples of very well-known textual interest, can be bought for about one-twentieth of the price of the first editions. The fact is, of course, that serials, especially in newspapers, are very awkward things to shelve as well as being often extremely hard to find: so logic yields to convenience.

A final example of the inconsistencies which cataloguers catch by reflexion from their customers is provided by the once lively and still occasionally debated question whether first editions follow chronology or nationality. The 'follow the flag' controversy was discussed in our review of the thirties: [3] nothing useful has been, or is likely to be, added to the arguments then advanced by both sides: and it will be sufficient to note here that though the case for chronology remains logically unassailable, nothing will apparently induce more than 5 per cent of collectors to pay any attention to it. As the President of the Grolier Club (Mr Frederick B. Adams, Jr) recently observed: 'The aggregate whim of collectors is a whim of iron, cannot be governed by rules, and will always prefer *Moby Dick* to *The Whale*.' [4]

[1] 3 vols., 1894: previously serialised in *Harper's Magazine*.
[2] 3 vols., 1891; previously serialised in *The Graphic* and parts also in *The Fortnightly* and *The National Observer*.   [3] See above, p. 61.
[4] *One Hundred Influential American Books* (New York, Grolier Club, 1947), p. 16. The London edition of Melville's book was published earlier than the New York, under the title of *The Whale*.

The third type of confusion arises from discrepancies in the standard of connoisseurship between one rare book catalogue and another. This is at the same time the most vexatious to the collector, the easiest to excuse and the most difficult to reduce to order, no matter how much attention and goodwill is directed upon it. It is not sufficient to say that expert and responsible booksellers describe their books fairly, while knaves or fools mislead, and that the solution, for any collector not thoroughly confident of his own expertise, is to rely on the former and avoid the latter. This solution takes care of that small number of disreputable dealers and that larger, but still not large, number of incompetent ones. It does not touch the real root of the matter, which is the disparity between the terms employed by different booksellers of the utmost respectability for expressing the fine shades of condition among the books they are describing or the precise degree of rarity which they consider attributable to them.

The description of condition is the more important to the collector. He may accept or reject an estimate of rarity, but his decision whether to order a book will often depend on the fidelity with which its physical condition can be trusted to conform to a set of standards he may or may not share with the man who is describing it. Some booksellers he will know for their strictness, so that a book which is given no adjective at all may be safely presumed to be in good state: for if it were not, the cataloguer would have said so. Others he will remember as lenient fellows, prone to take a charitable view of cripples and to regard the scars left by library labels as, if not positively honourable, at least more tactfully ignored: and from them he will hardly consider ordering anything not described as 'brilliant' or better, unless in the expectation of getting what another would call 'fair'.[1]

---

[1] James Lackington (*Memoirs*, 1792 edition, p. 329) writes thus of his 1779 catalogue, issued in partnership with John Denis: 'Referring to certain scarce old mystical and alchymical books, printed above a century ago, many of them', he says, 'were in bad condition; this led him (Denis) to insert *neat* in the catalogue to many articles, which were only neat when compared with such as were in very bad condition; so that when we produced such books as were called *neat* in our catalogues, we often got ourselves laughed at, and sometimes our *neat* articles were heartily *damned*.'

Since we shall be considering the whole question of condition later, it must suffice to observe here that probably no two book-sellers of equal standing (nor any two collectors either, for that matter) would find their descriptions of a hundred selected books tally as to more than sixty or seventy; and that even if their eyes agreed on the remaining thirty or forty, their words would not. Poor, moderate or used? Fair, good or satisfactory? Excellent, very fine or choice? Brilliant, immaculate or 'as new'?—each man has his own nuances and can never be absolutely sure what to expect from another's epithet. We shall also be examining the factor of rarity. And in respect of this much more debatable quality in a book it is perhaps comforting to remember that the variety of terms used to measure it by cataloguers, while quite as luxuriant and unstandardised as those which describe condition, are the expression of opinion, not of fact. It is only human to take an optimistic view of something you own, but it is also human to take the word of a seller with a few grains of salt unless you know him. Most collectors, therefore, probably discount (often unconsciously) by at least one degree any estimate of rarity from an unfamiliar source. But they will be wise to defer to the opinion of a trusted expert when the question concerns a book of whose frequency of occur-rence they know little or nothing. It is much easier to tell a fine copy from a poor one than a rare book from a common. All that is needed for the former is a little experience and a pair of eyes. The latter requires not only much more experience but also a nose, which is a feature denied to many very conscientious and deserving book-collectors.

CHAPTER X

BOOKSHOP AND AUCTION ROOM

The auction room is the great leveller of all manner of unmerited fame. WILLIAM ROBERTS

Booksellers are various, good and bad, sly and frank, straight and crooked, wise, wayward, mean, generous, greedy, open-handed, proud, humble, quiet, noisy, well read and ill read, as other tradesmen are; but there is, I find, a numerous company of the best of them. HOLBROOK JACKSON

'ON your Shakespeare of 1623', wrote Thomas Rodd,[1] the London bookseller, to Thomas P. Barton, a collector in New York, in the middle of the last century, 'on your Shakespeare of 1623 I pin my reputation, moral as well as bibliographical. If you do not find it in every respect perfect and genuine, I will make you a present of the book, and will in addition forfeit ten pounds a leaf for every one that is not genuine.' Rodd's language is perhaps more flowery than would be employed today by Maggs or Francis Edwards, Rosenbach or Goodspeed: but his attitude towards his customer and his book differs only in degree, not in kind, from that of any honourable bookseller of his day or ours. The great dealers of Rodd's time were as good bookmen as their customers: taking a keen interest in their collections, fighting their battles in the auction room, scouring the British Isles and the Continent in their interest. Some, indeed, such as Longman and Pickering, were often more imaginative, acquiring stock and issuing catalogues in advance of the taste of their time, to their own financial detriment. They were not necessarily urbane or ingratiating characters (though the ambitious Foss might have offered Sir John Thorold a glass of sherry), and it is recorded[2] that Joseph Lilly's brusque and overbearing manner nearly alienated the diffident Henry Huth at the very beginning of a career which Lilly was subsequently to have so large a hand in forming.

[1] Quoted by Harry B. Smith in *The Colophon*, part 3 (1930).
[2] By F. S. Ellis in Quaritch's *Contributions towards a Dictionary of Book-Collectors* (1896).

The influence of Henry Stevens of Vermont and Obadiah Rich on the American collectors of mid-century has already been noted. The third quarter saw the rise of Bernard Quaritch, by common consent the greatest bookseller of his own, or perhaps any other, day. Quaritch, who was of German origin, entered the London book business in the forties and brought to it such a combination of enterprise, knowledge, courage and business ability that he dominated the later years of the century in most of the major fields of book-collecting of the older style: dying, it has been picturesquely said, with nothing in the bank and the finest stock in Europe. His energy and influence were particularly notable in the great series of Roxburghe-type sales of the eighties and nineties, which without his resolute support might well have flooded a market by then less universally receptive to this kind of material.

The traditions of expertise and integrity set by the principal booksellers of the nineteenth century have been worthily maintained, despite a few exceptions, in the twentieth. Bibliography as well as bibliophily owes a debt to such learned booksellers as Luther S. Livingston, Edgar H. Wells and James F. Drake in America, and in England to Charles Massey (of Pickering and Chatto), Thomas Stephenson (of Rimell and Son), A. W. Evans (of Elkin Mathews) and the late [1] lamented partnership of Birrell and Garnett. And how many Cambridge men laid sound foundations for a collecting career at old David's stall in the Market Place? The number must run into hundreds. Nor is it fitting that tribute should be withheld from the living: for it may be doubted whether the later seventeenth century can claim a more devoted expert than Mr Percy Dobell, the study of early printing than Mr Lathrop Harper, the Renaissance in all its aspects than Mr E. P. Goldschmidt or the *STC* period than Mr F. S. Ferguson, for many years custodian of the Quaritch tradition in Grafton Street. Mr Dudley Massey, one of the best judges of a book in London, will surely be

---

[1] 'Late,' only to the book-trade: for though the firm closed its doors in 1942, all its successive directors except Francis Birrell—Mr David Garnett, Mr Ralph Wright, Mr Graham Pollard and Miss J. E. Norton—now decorate other fortunate professions.

conceded to be a chip off the old block; while Mr Percy Muir, maintaining to the full the Elkin Mathews spirit and momentum, is also a prolific and effective bibliographical propagandist.

There was, indeed, cause for apprehension in the twenties, when stock-market tactics were introduced into the book business on both sides of the Atlantic. In New York, particularly, a group of *arriviste* dealers hurried to assume patches from the mantle of George D. Smith: that tremendous buccaneer who had singed the beard of every reverend signior in Europe in the interests of Huntington and other customers, and had taught his countrymen that the principle of *toujours l'audace* could be as effective in the auction room as in other fields of warlike diplomacy. Some of these men were not so much booksellers as financial operators in the book-market, as were some of the collectors whom they served; and though they mostly disappeared along with the conditions in which such operations thrive, the book-trade as a whole proved not entirely immune from the infection of their methods. The chastening thirties did much to redress the damage, for they made a necessity of virtue. But it remains to be seen whether another boom can be weathered without developing shock-tactics, speculation and 'merchandising': a question to which the answer lies as much in the hands of collectors as of booksellers.

In general, however, the peculiarly intimate relationship between bookseller and collector has not merely survived unimpaired the strains and stresses of the past quarter of a century. It has in some ways been intensified. For if integrity is an absolute quality, expertise is relative. And if the collector must always rely on the former in a steady measure, he has to rely more heavily on the latter with every decade's increase in special knowledge and connoisseurship. A bookseller may be as honest as the day, but if he does not know that the Aldine *Poliphilus* (Venice, 1499) needs a leaf of errata, that there is a secondary binding of *The Ordeal of Richard Feverel* (3 vols., 1859), that a half-title is called for in the second volume of Adam Smith's *Wealth of Nations* (1776) but not in the first—to take three points which in fact every bookseller does know—he may in all good faith sell you a wrong book. Of course he will take it back if *you* know. But collectors cannot know everything. As often as not they must ask not only 'is this an honest copy?' but also 'is it right?'

The distinction between ethics and expertise was clearly present in the mind of Thomas Rodd when he pledged his reputation 'moral as well as bibliographical'. And the necessity for confidence in both has more recently been stated, perhaps in a rather extreme form, but certainly with a salutary emphasis, by Messrs Winterich and Randall.[1] 'If the collector [they maintain] cannot find a dealer in whose complete honesty and judgment he can place as much faith as he does, say, in that of his doctor, lawyer or minister, he had better stop collecting. For neither he nor the dealer will have any fun. Collecting is a two-way street, and the rare book dealer of integrity who feels that a particular collector does not have faith in him (despite, perhaps, an occasional unwitting error) will cheerfully give up that collector.' It is here recognised that the most expert booksellers are liable to error, like the rest of mankind; but it is well also for the collector to be reminded that his intimate relationship with his bookseller carries obligations as well as privileges. It is the honourable dealer's pleasure and pride, no less than his duty and his business, to foster the collections of his customers. He tries to be worthy of their confidence: but he has a right to some confidence in return. A suspicious or a grudging collector brings out the worst in his bookseller; and if it is natural for the ignorant to be more suspicious than the experienced—really ignorant collectors are usually either criminally credulous or absurdly suspicious—the veterans have less excuse. For they know enough about collecting to have confidence in their own judgment in cases where they withhold confidence from the dealer's, and they should know enough about human nature to realise how heavily a suspicious attitude to any dealer's books and a grudging attitude towards his prices handicaps them in their collecting. No bookseller resents a reasoned scepticism in bibliographical matters, nor an honest difference of opinion as to the value of a book. Indeed, a good bookseller respects, appreciates and is glad to profit by both, when they are backed by knowledge and experience. What he does resent is a collector who regularly assumes that he is about to be

[1] Op. cit., p. 187.

deceived and automatically regards a marked price as something to be reduced. He will sell to such a one reluctantly and with a sour heart. For though booksellers are destined always to be parting from books, they have a liking for them and a pride in their own stock. The grocer who sells a pound of butter cares nothing who eats it. But the bookseller who has a fine thing to dispose of would rather sell it to someone who will appreciate it, whose collection is worthy of it and whose pleasure in the transaction can be shared by both parties to it. Since booksellers have to live, like other men, they cannot always pick and choose. A sale is a sale, even if it is made with a sigh. But the customer who prides himself on being 'tough' would be surprised if he knew how often a book which he wants, and is known to want, has been kept in a drawer during his visit, to be sold, sometimes for a smaller profit, to another in whose collection the bookseller has been encouraged to take a personal interest.

It is this unanimity of interest between collector and dealer which so sharply differentiates the function and atmosphere of the bookshop from those of the auction room. The auctioneer is, of course, interested in the general health of book-collecting, both in the very short view and in the very long view: for he has to get the best prices he can at today's session, and he would be glad to be reassured that there will be both a fine library to offer and a satisfactory attendance at its sale, in ten years' time. But his interest is inevitably an impartial one, since his first duty is to his consigners. It is as inevitably impersonal: for though he can, if he likes, solicit bids from individual collectors for individual books, he is selling something which he has not himself bought, so that his offerings reflect a borrowed, sometimes an alien, personality. And between sales there is little to maintain his relationship with the collector, which is therefore fitful as well as oblique, where the bookseller's is close, continuous and direct. An important sale strikes sparks from the collecting world and the rostrum is vividly, though momentarily, high-lighted. But it is the constant and fostering care of the bookseller which maintains the collector at or near the sparking temperature.

To stress the essential difference of these two functions is by no means to depreciate the importance of the auction room to collectors and dealers alike. Quite the contrary. Sales are a vital component in the machinery of book-collecting, and the great auction houses lend a colour, an excitement and a romance to the business of dispersal and acquisition, which is as welcome to the trade as it is stimulating to the collector. If Dibdin could speak of that 'delightful thrill, never to be duplicated', and if Horace Walpole left the House of Commons during a debate to attend a book sale,[1] it was Dr Rosenbach, the bookseller, who observed[2] that the auction room 'calls forth courage, promptness, and the spirit of adventure', maintaining that 'of all branches of the sport, that of attending book auctions is the greatest, the most stirring'. But whereas the bookseller is under no temptation to usurp the auctioneer's function, since he has not the means even if he had the will, the auctioneers of New York have for a couple of decades past been moving into the territory of the dealers, so that the distinction of function has tended, in America at any rate, to become blurred.[3]

In the last century and the early years of the present (as to a strictly limited extent still in England today) a book-auction was really a wholesaling operation: the retailing being done by the booksellers, who solicited and handled their customers' bids but also bought largely for stock. Private collectors were not encouraged to bid in person and seldom did so, preferring to entrust their ventures to their agents, whose expert assistance first in appraising, then in securing and finally in collating the book they thus enlisted, in return for a commission of 10 per cent, or sometimes less. This practice suited the auctioneer for several reasons. The purchasers were commonly dealers of established status, to whom he could give credit without question. They were also

[1] Holbrook Jackson, op. cit., p. 599.
[2] *Books and Bidders*, p. 75.
[3] Continental practice is quite different. In some countries the bookseller is the sole exponent of the auctioneer's function: in others he periodically assumes it.

reasonably expert, so that unnoticed faults in a book would be exposed before rather than after the fall of the hammer, thus minimising the troublesome business of returns. But most important of all, the preponderance of professional over private bidding gave a stability to prices which the dealers had a real and personal interest in maintaining, in bad times as in good. Even the bookseller is not wholly proof against the psychology of the auction room: but he will neither bid himself, nor encourage any customer for whom he is acting to bid, a price grossly in excess of what he deems a book to be worth. He knows that fancy prices are bad for the book business in the long run, and that if he buys a book for twice what it is worth this month his professional reputation will be, in some measure at least, involved when another copy turns up next month. Private collectors have no such concern. When money is plentiful they will throw it about in the auction room as they would never do in a bookshop. But when times are bad, it is no business of theirs if a hundred pound book goes for a fiver. And in a market where most prices are, after all, artificial, the impression that the same book can have a widely different value in different sets of circumstances is as dangerous to the wellbeing of collectors and auctioneers as it is to booksellers.

Apart from the fact that many people get a little drunk with the excitement of the auction room, the idea is still prevalent among collectors that auction prices are always cheaper than bookshop prices. This was perhaps apt to be the case in the days when auction prices were more nearly wholesale than retail in character and when one's opponent was a bookseller bidding for stock. It was never true when he was bidding on commission, and it is seldom true at all today in the major sale rooms of London and New York, whether the opposing bid be on commission or for stock. It is, therefore, fallacious to suppose that just because someone else was willing to bid only one unit less than what the book is knocked down for, it is of necessity a bargain. On a falling market it may be, or at a small country sale, or if it is a common book with an established price, on which a dealer would make little profit anyway and none if he seriously overbid his mark. But in general a collector bidding in person is likely to pay as much as, and sometimes more than, he would have done if he had given his bid to his bookseller or bought the item from a bookshop. To grudge the dealer his commission, as the unthinking or the mean do, is like dispensing with an architect for your house. On a small, fool-proof operation a little money may be saved: on anything considerable it will sometimes be an expensive economy. For there is much more to the execution of a commission for a customer than a readiness to nod to the auctioneer more persistently than another.

Anyone who considers 10 per cent a high price to pay for a bookseller's expertise[1] should read the conditions of sale printed in all auction catalogues. He will be surprised by the almost complete disclaimer of any warranty whatsoever in respect of the goods to be offered. Unless he is prepared not only to inspect but to collate the book he wants, in advance, and unless he knows himself better qualified than his bookseller to do so, he may consider his bibliographical insurance alone cheap at the price. But in addition he will have had his bookseller's advice, if he wants it, on what this copy is worth, and also on what it may be expected to fetch in this particular sale, which is often something quite different. And finally he will have the services of an expert in the actual landing of the book, a proceeding sometimes calling for the nicest judgment.

The diffident private bidder is always a trifle flurried. Not only is he the cynosure of the room, but he is also trying feverishly to identify the bidder against him. This is instinctive, and he would often be none the wiser for the knowledge. In fact, of course, if his opponent is a dealer, he will probably, having once caught the auctioneer's attention, be bidding with his eyebrow or by raising his pencil. If the other bid is at the desk, our poor friend will feel that he is boxing with shadows, and after three or four raises he will not know which is his bid and which the auctioneer's. It is at this point that an unscrupulous auctioneer (and they do exist) will either let the collector bid himself up or, when that fails, will 'pick

[1] Although this point has not been tested in the courts, the English laws of warranty do not commit the accepter of a commission to bid to any guarantees in respect of the object bid for, beyond what the auctioneer himself warrants. But in practice the collector expects, and normally gets, whatever protection from error his bookseller's abilities and effort can afford him.

a bid off the wall', as the phrase is, to raise him another notch or two. No self-confident person, of course, would be thus put about. He will bid boldly, and show his hand; or he will think to come in triumphantly at the end, and have the book knocked down elsewhere while he is still holding his fire; or he will mistake another collector for a dealer and assume that he can safely go one higher, until he has paid far more than his book is worth.

At the other end of the scale, a specialist well known to the trade is at a particular disadvantage, no matter how well he may know the ropes. For if he bids on a clearly recognised lot, dealers will pay him the left-handed compliment of trying to outbid him simply because they think he knows the book better than they do; while if he bids on a bundle he focuses attention on something presumably in it, which might otherwise have been overlooked. The great Thorn-Drury was once (so they say) bid up on a miscellaneous lot from the ten shillings at which it was ready to fall, to twenty-nine pounds, at which he retired, only to be thereupon asked by the buyer what was in the bundle.

These are slightly exaggerated pictures: but only slightly. And even if the collector is neither diffident nor over-confident, nor a conspicuous expert, he will often conclude that his bookseller knows the angles better than he can ever expect to do. For an old auction-room hand has a shrewd idea which booksellers are likely to be seriously interested in which lots: he knows from long experience what deductions can be drawn from the way they are bidding: he will probably have developed a sixth sense for a strong commission elsewhere in the room, and will handle his own bidding accordingly. Playing a bid is like playing a fish. An air of reluctance, even of disinterest, will be successful with one lot, while a resolute, money-no-object opening may on another occasion discourage competition and secure the book well below one's mark. This sounds a fascinating game, and so it is. But it is a game for professionals, not amateurs.

This opinion would probably be endorsed by most English auctioneers, who believe in a predominantly professional *clientèle*, for reasons already propounded. Their sales are conducted, their catalogues prepared and their advertising devised accordingly. They accept private bids, but they seldom solicit them. They admit the loud-speaker and the news cameras on a great occasion, but the normal sale is a subdued gathering of quiet men round a dingy green baize table. They will sometimes spread themselves over the description of a spectacular book, but their catalogues are commonly stripped to the bare essentials (and sometimes further), on the assumption that they are provided for professionals, not the uninstructed, and furthermore that the function of an auction-catalogue is accurate description and not ballyhoo.

New York's practice is different because its policy is different. The one major auction house in the city has deliberately set itself to attract direct collector-custom and it conducts its operations accordingly. Even in the days before this policy was adopted, American sales were held in a very different style from London's: usually in the evening, with a fashionable crowd at any important dispersal; comfortable chairs, and uniformed staff calling bids for the auctioneer; a spotlight on the lot selling, which is reverently displayed on a dais (no passing round the table); in short, an atmosphere eminently conducive to the painless extraction of that extra bid. This technique has proved very effective, and if the dealers are sufficiently habituated to be immune, the public are not. Cataloguing style follows the same pattern. Descriptions of condition are much fuller, which benefits the out-of-town dealer as well as the collector, and must be generally considered a very advantageous contrast, so long as the descriptions are accurate, to the tight-lipped manner of London. But the entries are not con-fined to description. They are freely garnished with puffs of one kind and another, and it is this consciously promotional character which distinguishes them so clearly from the English variety. They often read more like a bookseller's catalogue than an auctioneer's exposition of consigned goods, and that is exactly what, essentially, they are: for they are not so much designed to describe books for booksellers as to sell them to collectors.

Now this ambition, which is furthered by correspondence and personal contacts, is an entirely proper one in itself: judged, that is, without relation to book-collecting as a whole. It also has a plausible sound: cut out the middleman, and the owner gets more money while the buyer pays less. But it remains to be seen whether it can be fully achieved, in New York or anywhere else, without doing such harm to the delicate and complex structure of the book-business as will eventually react just as sharply on its proponents as on the retailers whom they are willing to by-pass. It has always been supposed (and has been taken for granted earlier in this chapter) that an auction house needed both the steady support of the trade, buying for stock as well as on commission, and the support of a widely spread body of regular collectors, such as cannot be maintained, let alone guided and cherished, by the offerings and efforts of any auctioneer independently of the booksellers.

Only time will tell whether an auction house can live on an autarkic diet, supplemented by such business as dealers must do there when they cannot do it anywhere else. The most notable outcome of this policy to date, in the general area of collecting technique, is just what might have been (and probably was) predicted: a substantial crop of collectors who buy only at auction and never from a bookseller's shelves, even though they may (as many do) employ a bookseller to execute their commissions. Many of these gentlemen have assembled considerable collections, which they undoubtedly suppose themselves to have acquired for less money than the same books would have cost them in bookshops. While it is permissible to doubt this, no one can prove it one way or the other; and indeed it should perhaps be conceded to them, as a consolation for all the other books which they might have found—or, who knows, been offered—if they had not so drastically limited their field of vision.

Most fully fledged collectors, of course, like to keep an eye on the auction sale catalogues, even though they may rely on their regular bookseller (or one of several regulars) to draw their attention to material in which they are known to be interested. A few busy men are further content to delegate to

him the scrutiny, for their special subjects, of some at least of
the innumerable minor booksellers' catalogues which tend to
pile up on their study tables; though the real *aficionado* will
hardly let the sun go down on an unread list, no matter how
humble, for fear he may find himself reaching for the telephone
a day too late. It is, moreover, a not uncommon practice, and
one seldom resented in the trade unless it is abused, for a collector to channel an order from an unfamiliar catalogue through
his regular bookseller, in order to get the benefit of advice he
knows he can rely on, to avoid multiplying accounts, or even
perhaps simply to save himself trouble. The dealer in such cases
is usually ready enough to keep his customer (as he not always
accurately supposes) from straying too far afield, and in return
for the customary 10% discount between members of the trade
he gives the same service as he would to an auction commission.

Booksellers' catalogues are almost as various as the books
they list, both in matter and in manner. The often stylish productions of the West End dealers, like their elegant salons, are
designed primarily for collectors of a certain substance; and
both have been known to frighten those of humbler spirit or
circumstances. Yet any true collector is sure of a welcome from
any good bookseller, no matter what the economic brackets
within which they may do business; and the collector who
neglects a glossy catalogue or glossy premises from timidity is
as foolish as the other who is too grand to bother with the six-
penny box or the mimeographed list. It is experience, not face
values, that will teach him whose catalogues he can probably
afford to skip, whose basement ignore. He can never be quite
certain, of course: but catalogues, like booksellers and their shops,
have their own flavour and style, which most collectors learn
pretty quickly to recognise as sympathetic or not to their own
tastes and interests. Real veterans sometimes develop a positively
uncanny nose for good books in hopelessly unpromising places—
and this is several stages further than just unlikely places, for
no one will be surprised to see the collector of Stevenson in the
'Forestry' section or the devotee of Charles Reade at the shelves
marked 'Musical Instruments'. The old hand will similarly write

off in short order the unseen portions of the establishment which sports a lot of glass-fronted locked cabinets full of sophisticated copies of *demodés* first editions at inflated prices.

There has inevitably been a good deal of talk in this book about prices. And it will perhaps be not inappropriate to conclude a chapter about buying and selling with a word or two about prices in general. Let us then, as usual, take Pollard for our text.[1] 'While largely influenced by fashion [he writes] the prices given for books are never wholly unreasonable. They are determined, firstly by the positive or associative interest which can be found in the book itself, secondly by the infrequency with which copies come into the market compared with the number and wealth of their would-be possessors, and thirdly, except in the case of books of the greatest interest and rarity, by the condition of the copy offered in respect to completeness, size, freshness and absence of stains.'

His concluding words show that Pollard was thinking principally of early books. But his general diagnosis applies pretty well to more modern books too. Unfortunately, however, what most collectors want is not so much diagnosis as prescription: a short simple formula for telling whether such and such a book is too dear, dear but probably not to be let pass, fairly priced, cheap but perhaps hardly a good enough copy even at that price, or finally a 'sitter' or 'sleeper', as the booksellers call a real bargain. There is, of course, no such formula. The collector will have to learn about prices by the hard way of experience, though he may assist himself by studying sales records and booksellers' catalogues and by enquiry among his fellow-collectors.

I will venture, however, to suggest a few general principles. *First*, auction records are most unreliable guides unless full account is taken of the quality of the copy (seldom deducible from the annual summaries), the date (whether in a period of high or low prices) and the character of the sale (pedigree sales make higher prices even for the minor books than miscellaneous sales). *Secondly*, a cheap mediocre copy is probably more expensive than a high-

[1] Loc. cit.

priced but brilliant example of the same book. *Thirdly*, the collector must expect to pay a little more for a book which is reported to him than for one which he digs out: he is paying for the bookseller's time, trouble and memory. *Fourthly*, it is unreasonable to expect a bookseller who has bought a bargain to forgo his profit simply because his purchase price is known to his customer, or to sell for a 10 per cent profit what he invested his own money in (not his customer's) at an auction. *Fifthly*, books are by no means always dearer in the West End of London than in the suburbs or the provinces (and the same goes for New York). 'Bargains', said Hazlitt,[1] 'may be obtained off the counters of the most acute'; and while this is still true, it is even truer that a book of known consequence is often more reasonably, because less excitedly, priced in Bond Street than in Bootle. *Sixthly*, real howling bargains are very rare. They should never be reckoned on or waited for, or one may wait for ever. The best purchases most collectors make are due to prescience, not good fortune: they are the books bought at a fair market price ten years, five years, perhaps even only one year before enough other people are looking for them to send the price up. *Seventhly*, if a collector is in doubt whether a certain book for which he has been looking is not, when he finds it, over-priced, let him consider the bookseller's probable attitude towards that particular book. Some booksellers over-price from ignorance, others from knowledge abetted by a belief that the book is rarer or more important than has been generally supposed. *Eighthly*, never bargain. If you succeed in beating the bookseller down on this book, you will have saved a little money. But will he offer you the next one he knows you want?[2] A marked price is a dealer's honest opinion. You are fully entitled to disagree with him and to say so. But you should take the book or leave it. If you leave it and he is right, someone else will get it. He may, of course, be wrong. If so, the book will stay with him and he will probably

---

[1] Op. cit., p. 94.

[2] Holbrook Jackson (op. cit., p. 604) quotes Selden's *Table-Talk* for the thesis that the 'giving of a bookseller his price for his books has this advantage, he that will do so shall have the refusal of whatsoever comes to his hand, and so by that means get many things, which otherwise he never would have seen. So 'tis in giving a bawd her price.'

meet you of his own accord after a decent interval. *Ninthly*, never think, when you are buying a book, what it will sell for—tomorrow or fifty years hence. As Messrs Winterich and Randall[1] have well said: 'A man who considers books primarily as investments or speculations is not a collector. He is in the book business.... No man can serve two masters, and no wise man tries.'

Tenthly, and lastly, be less afraid of paying a stiff price than of letting slip some book you know to be rare and which is important to you. You cannot tell when, at what price, or even whether, you will see another. De Ricci expressed this principle in an eloquent passage[2] which shall serve for my peroration. 'Out-bidding [he cried] is the very essence of collecting. The most sacred duty of every collector is to overpay. To outbid and overpay is not a calamity, but an absolute necessity. But you can outbid by six-pence,[3] and many an item has been overpaid at half a crown if your closest rival valued it at only a florin. You will never be successful as a collector if you are not prepared to outbid and to overpay—let us say if you are not delighted to pay eighteen pence for a shilling item.

'Every great collection in the world, ever since there have been collectors, has been made by men who had foresight enough to secure for themselves, to snatch away from others, objects that they understood to be really significant and desirable. You must there-fore be prepared not only to outbid your competitors, but also to outwit them. "All is fair", says the proverb, "in love and war." Collecting, we will most of us admit, partakes both of love and war.'

[1] Op. cit., p. 194.
[2] *The Colophon*, no. 2 (1930).
[3] I have translated into English currency in this paragraph.

CHAPTER XI

RARITY

Every collector will find that some books are commoner than might reasonably be expected and some decidedly rarer. RICHARD CURLE

ATTEMPTS have from time to time been made to reduce the degrees of rarity in books to some sort of formula. David Clement, a distinguished French bibliographer of the eighteenth century, laid it down[1] that 'a book which it is difficult to find in the country where it is sought ought to be called simply *rare*; a book which is difficult to find in any country may be called *very rare*; a book of which there are only fifty or sixty copies existing, or which appears so seldom as to suggest that there never had been more at any time than that number of copies, ranks as *extremely rare*; and when the whole number of copies does not exceed ten, this constitutes *excessive rarity*, or *rarity in the highest degree*'.

This classification was condemned by Burton, a century later, as 'utter pedantry'. 'Books', he continues, 'may be rare enough in the real or objective sense of the term, but if they are not so in the nominal or subjective sense, by being sought after, their rarity goes for nothing. A volume may be unique—may stand quite alone in the world—but whether it is so, or one of a numerous family, is never known, for no one has ever desired to possess it.'

Burton's condemnation may be too sweeping, just as Clement's hierarchy is clearly too rigid. But the difference of underlying principle brings us at once to grips with the real problem of rarity, which will be remembered as one of the essential ingredients of Pollard's definition of book-collecting, notwithstanding his warning that its weight is often overestimated in the popular conception. For there are several distinct kinds of rarity, each with its subdivisions: and among them are absolute rarity, relative or comparative rarity, localised rarity, and temporary rarity.

[1] Quoted (and presumably translated) by Burton, op. cit., p. 210. Italics mine.

Absolute rarity is a property possessed by any book which is printed in an extremely short number: one of which therefore the total of potentially surviving copies is definitely known and known to be very small. Of Tennyson's *The Lover's Tale* (1833), for example, only six copies were done, and the same number of Swinburne's *Siena* (1868). Archdeacon Wrangham was fond of having a handful of copies taken off on pink or green paper,[1] just as Aldus did on blue 300 years earlier. And we are all familiar with that calculated limitation which, though not peculiar to any one country, achieves its finest flowering in the *justification du tirage* of a modern French illustrated book. It is not strictly just to say, with Slater,[2] that 'books extensively advertised as being issued in limited editions should be avoided, for no publisher would appeal to a small audience if he were sure of a large one', since there are often honourable reasons for the small size of an edition printed by hand; and Hazlitt[3] is perhaps too severe when he brands the *édition de luxe* as 'dilettantism *in extremis*'. But if some collectors, like Archdeacon Wrangham himself, love a rare book just because it is rare, and therefore difficult to find, nevertheless Burton was right at bottom. For absolute or any other kind of rarity lacks significance without demand, and a single copy of a book is more than enough if no one wants it.

Relative rarity is a property only indirectly connected with the number of copies of a book originally printed. It is based on the number which survive; but its practical test is the frequency or infrequency of occurrence in the market, and its practical interest (to any except statisticians) is the relation of this frequency to public demand. Of Thomas J. Wise's *Verses* (1882), for instance, the vellum issue has absolute rarity, for only five copies were so printed. Of the regular issue not many copies seem to have survived, so that its relative rarity is considerable; but since the

[1] Cf. Michael Sadleir, *Archdeacon Wrangham* (Bibliographical Society, Supplement no. 12, 1937).
[2] J. H. Slater, *How to Collect Books* (1905), p. 184.
[3] Op. cit., p. 191.

demand for the first edition is negligible, the degree of its in-frequency of occurrence is of small practical interest.

In the upper strata of relative rarity there are, certainly, degrees which approximate to the absolute. A book that has for a long period—say fifty years—made very infrequent appearances in spite of a steadily high reputation among collectors will eventually achieve a level of rarity which, whether extreme or not, is at least reasonably stable. It may even deserve that misused description 'so rare as to be virtually unprocurable'. We have seen, for instance, that the first editions of Shakespeare have for more than a century been the object of some, and for more than half a century of a very violent, interest. When this fact is related to the initially high destruction rate of flimsy and ephemeral produc-tions and their subsequent neglect for nearly two centuries, we are today justified in stating flatly that the early quartos are very rare indeed. It is possible that a third copy of the 1603 *Hamlet* may be unearthed tomorrow. But only two, both imperfect, are known to survive, and though a battery of eyes have long been trained on every volume of Elizabethan plays or pamphlets that turns up, no other has been found in more than a hundred years.

It is equally possible, but almost equally improbable, that any considerable addition to the recorded number of copies of the Caxton *Chaucer* (Westminster, 1478) or the *42-line Bible* (Mainz, ?1455) or Villon's *Grant Testament* (Paris, 1489) will now be made: so that the present degree of rarity of these and a small handful of kindred books can be assessed with only a small margin of error. It is, that is to say, nearly absolute. There are of course many books both important and sought after that are recorded as extant today in a far smaller number than the *42-line Bible*, but which yet have a better chance of increase to that number in the future. For they have not been subjected over a prolonged period to the tremendous suction exerted by a great and widely publicised esteem and a very high price.

It was observed above that rarity of occurrence is the practical test. And in this connection we must take full account of what has been called[1] 'the inevitable operation of that rider to the law of gravity whereby every important example of literary or artistic property is destined one day to inclusion in an institutional collection'. We have seen that many of the great eighteenth-century English collections, and not a few later ones, have come to rest in public or university libraries. In America, the public-spirited tradition of Lenox and Brown has never died; and the impulse which moved Huntington and Folger, Clements and Chapin, to dignify their country, their state or their university with a monument worthily honouring their own names has of recent years been fortified by the activity of the tax-collector. Even of those many great collections which have been, and will continue to be, dispersed by sale, some portions are always bought by or for institutional libraries. The number of desirable books, therefore, that are withdrawn from any reasonable possibility[2] of further circulation becomes continually greater every year; and although hard times or changed conditions as continually bring into the market libraries—monastic, ducal, or even, as in Germany and Russia, royal and imperial—which were once regarded as inviolable, it may be doubted whether even these sometimes substantial windfalls have kept pace with institutional absorption. 'The night of time', as Sir Thomas Browne said, 'far surpasseth the day, and who knows when was the equinox?'

To the average collector, however, even if he has ample means, these considerations apply rather in the general than in the particular sense, in that this remorseless withdrawal of books which are both important and rare progressively limits the top-soil available for cultivation by a newcomer and drives him to fresh fields: an often advantageous process which we have already discussed. His principal interest in rarity as a factor in book-collecting is of a more

[1] Winterich and Randall, op. cit., p. 196.

[2] Lincoln Cathedral Library, whose Caxtons were sold by private (very private) treaty twenty years ago, might be considered an institutional library; and the Drexel Institute of Philadelphia sold a section of its library in 1945. But such cases are rare. And while some public libraries are allowed by their constitutions to dispose of duplicates, this is a mere trickle back into the pool.

practical kind, and may be summed up in the elementary questions: which books are rare, and why?

We distinguished above between relative and temporary rarity; and since both are involved in any attempted answer to these questions, it will be convenient to deal first with the second and simpler of the two. *Temporary rarity*, then, depends directly on the laws of supply and demand. A change of taste or a new discovery stimulates interest among collectors in a book or a category of books hitherto not much regarded; the copies available are snapped up; and until the flow of supply gets under way through the regular channels, a temporary scarcity results, often accompanied by an artificially high price. It is of course notorious that a high price, well advertised, draws books out of their hiding places, whether in the maid's bedroom or the squire's study. As William Roberts[1] put it, 'The greater part of books do not die, but exist in a state of suspended animation, while they happen to be the class of literature for which the rulers of the market [collectors, one wonders, or booksellers?] are not immediately calling.' What is not so generally appreciated is the number of *comparatively* unregarded books on the upper shelves of collectors themselves and still more in the basements of booksellers. A dealer does not forget a hundred pound or even a five pound book in his stock: but he has too many five shilling books to remember them all; and it is an increased interest or a higher price that will remind him of some particular book, or will cause him to be asked for it, thus bringing into circulation unexpected copies and helping to redress the condition of temporary rarity.

Twenty years ago Hume's *Treatise on Human Nature* (3 vols., 1739–41) and Keats's *Poems* (1817) in boards were considered very rare books. Neither, certainly, is at all common today. But in response to a steady demand and, in the case of the former, a sharp increase in price, they now turn up more often than they did. Again, in 1924 one of the most knowledgeable and accurate of London booksellers catalogued Housman's *A Shropshire Lad* (1896) with the note that 'this and Mr de la Mare's *Songs of Childhood* (1902) are so rare as to be almost unprocurable'. So perhaps they

[1] *Rare Books and their Prices* (1895), p. 4.

then were, for the demand for them was still comparatively young. But for fifteen years past both have been common enough, though experience has shown that the latter, which had small initial success, is not infrequently found in clean condition, while the former, which was much read by its small but devoted public, is apt to be what the booksellers call 'used'.

It should be noted, in conclusion, that temporary rarity may sometimes, and most confusingly, result from the drying-up of supplies of a book which has long been in regular demand and is therefore well known to the trade; which was not rare five years ago and will not be five years hence; but which is today. And *vice versa*. *The Vicar of Wakefield* (2 vols., Salisbury, 1766) was a scarce book in the teens and twenties of this century, was much more often seen in the thirties, and must now (1948) again be reckoned scarce. This particular fluctuation may repeat itself, or it may not. But similar cases can sometimes be more easily explained. The Erasmus edition of the *New Testament* in greek, for example, published at Basel in 1516, was a rare book from 1870 to 1920; it made much more frequent appearances during the next fifteen years; and it has now relapsed into what will probably prove to be permanent rarity. For the influx of copies derived from those central European monastic libraries which were depleted after the First World War, and is never likely to be repeated.

In *localised rarity* the factor of geography is sometimes alternative to, but is more often superimposed upon, that of time. It is in many cases dissolved—obviously, though sometimes much more obstinately—in the same sort of way. Localised rarity may be illustrated, in its simplest form, by the observation that the first edition of *Madame Bovary* (Paris, 2 vols., 1857) is of much less frequent occurrence in England or America than in France. This is because it has been and still is less widely or energetically collected in either country than in that of its origin and main original circulation. Since, however, being an internationally famous book, it has of recent years attracted a respectable number of English and American collectors, copies do appear now and then; it is a 'known book' among dealers and the gossips; and the *cognoscenti* at least have a fair idea of its world rarity. Of the rarity of Ludovic

Halévy's *Une Maladresse*, by contrast, a book published in the same city in the same year, a Parisian *amateur* would doubtless be well informed: but one might expect to search the English-speaking countries in vain for an expert opinion, since the book has never been seriously, if at all, collected there. It would certainly be safe to pronounce it very rare indeed on this side of the Channel, but for all our experience can tell us it might be as common as *Felix Holt* on the other.[1]

It will always remain broadly true that copies of any book additional to those in bibliophilic circulation are more likely to turn up, not necessarily in its place or even its country of origin, but in the area of its original distribution. For a Venetian or Nuremberg incunable in latin, an Aldine or Elzevir or Plantin classic, this area would be coterminous with literate Europe, while for a vernacular treatise printed at Deventer in 1480 it would not extend much beyond the Low Countries. Baskerville's *Ariosto* (4 vols., Birmingham, 1773) is perhaps as likely to turn up in Parma as Bodoni's *Gray* (Parma, 1793) in Birmingham; but Smart's *A Song to David* (1763) or *Lady Audley's Secret* (3 vols., 1862) would be as unexpected a find in Lyons as *Tartuffe* (Paris, 1669) or Heine's *Buch der Lieder* (Hamburg, 1827) in Aberdeen.

Such general expectations, however, will be modified by the warmth and the geographical extent of the esteem enjoyed by the book concerned in the past. For the resultant suction will have brought many of the available copies into circulation; and an ever-increasing proportion of the residue will be lurking in unsuspected corners outside the area of search. The Folger copy of the First Quarto *Titus Andronicus* (1594), it will be remembered, was discovered not in England but in Sweden; and if an unrecorded example of one of John Heywood's plays or of the March issue of the 1549 *Prayer Book* or a collection of Marprelate tracts were to be unearthed tomorrow, it is just as likely that it would be in Bruges as in Bloomsbury. But if the *Complutensian Polyglot* (Alcalà, 1514–17) is not necessarily any commoner in Spain than in Poland, the original editions of *War and Peace* (Moscow, 1864–9) and *The*

---

[1] Actually it is nothing of the kind: cf. Carteret, *Trésor du Bibliophile* (Paris, 1924), vol. I, p. 370.

Brothers Karamazov (Moscow, 1879–80), of Hans Andersen's *Fairy Tales* (Copenhagen, 1835–7), of Schopenhauer's *The World as Will and Idea* (Leipzig, 1819), will probably remain, at least for some decades to come, less desperately rare in their native countries than elsewhere.

The great body of books of more localised reputation than these will naturally remain rarer of occurrence outside their own area of demand. Yet special cases of local rarity are constantly being created by some irregularity or freak of distributive procedure. If it is true that more copies of W. H. Auden's *Poems*, published in London in 1930, were sold by one bookseller in New York than by all the booksellers in what was then the author's own country, it is probably now commoner in the United States than in England. And an extreme example is provided by the first French translation (*Nuit sans Lune*, 1942) of John Steinbeck's novel, *The Moon is Down*, which was printed in London in miniature format for clandestine circulation in occupied France. Since the printing was 60,000 copies and the distribution methods of the Political Warfare experts uncommonly adroit, the book should be no great rarity on the Continent; but it may be doubted whether half a dozen could be found (outside the official files) in England and America combined. Fifty years of steady demand, however, would shift the centre of gravity of both books, in respect of *copies in circulation*, to the area where that demand was strongest.

Temporary rarity, then, to sum up, is no more than the short-term, and localised rarity the medium-term, inability of the machinery of supply to adjust itself to demand. But if the causes of the latter are obvious and the causes of the former often readily, and sometimes painfully, identifiable in retrospect, we must not be blind to the awkward fact that the early symptoms of either are often difficult to distinguish from those of real rarity. Supply will perhaps be inadequate to a newly evoked demand for, shall we say, first editions of Mrs Gore, or the cardinal documents in the history of atomic fission. And this may well be due only to the fact that these books have not been much sought after by collectors in the past and therefore have to be winkled out. On the other hand, they may turn out to be rarities in their own right, remaining so no matter how long and how hard they are looked for.

At the time when general collectors began to invade the fields of economics, politics and science, initial experience suggested that Helvetius's *De l'Esprit* (Paris, 1758) and Montesquieu's *L'Esprit des Lois* (2 vols., Geneva, 1748) were both hard books to find. We should now recognise the former (despite the story that it was burned by the public hangman) as common and the latter as rare, just as we now know, what we then had no particular reason to anticipate, that Bentham's *Principles of Morals and Legislation* (1789) is ten times rarer than Godwin's *Political Justice* (2 vols., 1793). Furthermore, an increased rarity which might reasonably be expected by the experts to be due to a mere dislocation in the regular appearance of a well-established book, may prove in the event to result from a permanent narrowing of the supply. And here long experience is apt to be a handicap: one is disposed to think, because Newton's *Principia Mathematica* (1687), for example, or the *editio princeps* of Sophocles (Venice, 1502) or Mrs Gaskell's *Life of Charlotte Brontë* (2 vols., 1857) were for years fairly common books, that they still are so; whereas each has apparently become scarce—or, shall we say, has now been of infrequent occurrence long enough to suggest that old estimates must be revised.

The collector faced with this dilemma realises that of the two questions which I put into his mouth—which books are rare, and why?—the second may become even more important than the first when he has passed through his novitiate and is ready to break new ground. For whereas a knowledge of relative rarities among books already in demand can be acquired, however laboriously, by experience, the probabilities of relative rarity among books not hitherto in demand can only be guessed at in the dim light of certain general principles inferred from that experience. Meanwhile observation will precede theory; first and foremost, of course, his own, but not neglecting that of others—the bibliographers or annotators of his subject, who may permit themselves some reflexions on the comparative rarity of individual books; fellow-collectors in his field; and, above all, the booksellers. As for these last, it is true that, on a short view, it is to the bookseller's advantage to represent his offerings in an attractive light, and that a facile asseveration of rarity may sometimes assist a single sale.[1] But any bookseller worth his salt sets much greater store by a steady customer and his own reputation as an expert than by any single sale. Consequently a seriously inaccurate attribution of rarity in a responsible dealer's catalogue is more often due to a fallacious tradition or to enthusiasm based on insufficient experience than to any wilful misrepresentation. The collector will very quickly learn from his own observations which booksellers are scrupulous in such matters, and furthermore which are reliable judges of which kinds of book, since dealers like collectors have their specialities. For instance, I should no more seek advice on James Joyce from Dr Ettinghausen or on Meredith from Mr Irving Davis than I should apply to Mr Rota or Mr Dudley Massey for an opinion on the relative scarcity of two *incunabula* printed in the same year at Naples: whereas I would adopt the contrary procedure with well-founded confidence. Yet even with this reservation, the general antiquarian bookseller's vast experience in the daily scanning and appraisal of miscellaneous collections gives him a sense of relative rarities far more extensive than any but the most exceptional collector can acquire.

There are admittedly a very great number of examples of un-explained disparities in observed rarity between books which from their date, size, appearance, circumstances of issue and literary reputation (both contemporary and subsequent) ought to have had equal chances of survival. I myself, for example, have been collecting the early editions of Catullus for more than a quarter of a century, during which time I have been (first for pleasure, later in the way of business) an assiduous reader of booksellers' and auctioneers' catalogues, English, Continental and American. And whereas I have seen, on an average, a couple of copies a year of the

---

[1] A friend of mine once found in a London bookshop an envelope containing more than twenty copies of some slender item, *each one of which* bore a note in the bookseller's hand: 'Very rare, the only copy we have ever seen.'

Aldine edition of 1502, I have never once seen—and therefore still lack—the Giunta edition of 1503. Brunet noted a century ago that the latter was the rarer of the two, but I was not prepared for so startling a difference. Catullus was a popular poet in the sixteenth century and was frequently reprinted, so that neither edition should have suffered punitively heavy wear. Both books are small octavos, well made, on good paper. It is true that Aldus's publishing organisation and the international prestige of his imprint gave his editions a better chance of wide distribution than those of any other Italian press at that time: yet the Giuntas were a substantial firm, enjoying a Papal privilege for the printing of the classics, and their books had a respectable contemporary market. It is true that Aldine editions were esteemed, and therefore preserved, by eighteenth- and nineteenth-century collectors, so that their survival ratio is high in proportion to their original numbers. Yet Giunta imprints too have been well thought of by later connoisseurs. In short, the only hypothesis that explains why the 1503 edition is now, as it certainly is, so very much rarer than the 1502, is that Aldus's original printing was very much larger than Giunta's.

If we turn to the first editions of seventeenth-century poetry, we shall not be surprised to find that Donne is much less rare than Vaughan, for he was a more popular writer and his editions were larger. The same reason no doubt accounts for the fact that the early editions of Herbert are today more easily found than those of Carew, and most titles of Waller and Cowley than either. But we may reasonably be surprised that Lovelace's *Lucasta* (1649) is today (though it seems not to have been in the nineteenth century) considerably rarer than Herrick's *Hesperides* (1648); for both were lyricists whose audience at the time might have been supposed approximately equal, and both books have been esteemed by collectors for many years. Being unable to account for the observed fact myself, I asked the opinion of several experts[1] in this period—booksellers, collectors, librarians and bibliographers—and here are their suggested explanations.

[1] Messrs P. J. Dobell, F. S. Ferguson, John Hayward, Richard Jennings, Hugh Macdonald, Kenneth Maggs, Dudley Massey, A. N. L. Munby, John Sparrow, Professor William A. Jackson and Colonel C. H. Wilkinson.

Only two factors were widely cited. A majority of my authorities (*a*) attributed *Hesperides*'s more numerous survival to its greater bulk—244 pages as against 97—and (*b*) suggested that a larger edition of it was printed. This latter is admittedly no more than a supposition: Mr Dudley Massey alone offering tentative support for it, in the fact that there are two states of a number of leaves and that some copies were published with an Exeter imprint. This, while it does not necessarily imply, is at least consistent with the hypothesis that the type was kept standing and possibly even reprinted from: but it is neutralised by Colonel Wilkinson's observation that a whole sheet was reprinted in *Lucasta*.

Mr Hayward points out that both poets were rather outmoded and that the original market for both books would have been a restricted one. (E. Marion Cox[1] says that *Hesperides* was popular at first, but soon dropped out of estimation.) Mr Munby remarks further that Lovelace had been both in prison and in financial straits, so that, literary merit apart, he might have been a less attractive proposition to a publisher. He notes that *Hesperides* was printed '*for* John Williams and Francis Eglesfield', *Lucasta* '*by* Tho. Harper *and are to be sold by* Tho. Ewster' (my italics in both), which suggests that whereas Herrick found a publisher, Lovelace may have published at his own or at a friend's expense. Professor Jackson drives this point home with the statement that Ewster was a relatively obscure bookseller, whose name is known in very few imprints, whereas Williams and Eglesfield were both well established. From this he deduces that *Lucasta* was less efficiently distributed; Colonel Wilkinson adds that it was still being advertised for sale in 1657; and Mr Hugh Macdonald hazards the possibility that the stock may have perished in the Great Fire.

Mr Dobell and Mr Hayward both remark on the long interval which elapsed before either book was reprinted (*Hesperides* 1810, *Lucasta* 1817): dismal evidence of the lack of public interest during a century and a half, which would adversely affect survival probability during that time, but affects both books equally. Mr Dobell

[1] *The Library*, vol. VIII (1917), p. 107.

and Mr Ferguson note the attraction for grangerisers of the two charming engravings in *Lucasta*. Both books often lack their frontispieces, it is true; but *Lucasta* is so tiny that grangerisers might well have thrown away what remained after their disgusting surgery was finished. Finally, Mr Massey and Mr Munby have established that although between 1850 and 1890 *Lucasta* was not so noticeably rarer than *Hesperides* as it has subsequently become— that is, both are found in the sort of libraries where they might be expected, such as Utterson, Daniel or Crawford—*Hesperides* was usually more expensive, because no doubt it was more admired. At auction, the Daniel copy in 1864 made £6. 10s. to *Lucasta*'s 36s., while Joseph Lilly the bookseller catalogued copies of the two at about the same time for £8. 8s. and £2. 12s. 6d. respectively. *Hesperides*, therefore, has been for at least a century more widely sought after and therefore probably better preserved.

None of these considerations, by itself, would suffice to explain the observed result. Cumulatively, however, they provide a tentative explanation. Their proponents, in the process, provided me with some profitable object-lessons. Yet it is a sobering thought that even among experts the factors on which an analysis of relative rarities depend must so often be a matter of hypothesis rather than of hard evidence.

Turning to a later date, one asks in vain why Bulwer Lytton's *Maltravers* (3 vols., 1837) and *Alice* (3 vols., 1838) should be so rare in any state compared with *The Last Days of Pompeii* (3 vols., 1834); why Meredith's *Harry Richmond* (3 vols., 1871) should be so much rarer in presentable condition than the novels on each side of it (*Vittoria*, 3 vols., 1867, and *Beauchamp's Career*, 3 vols., 1876); why Disraeli's *Venetia* (3 vols., 1837) in boards should be so uncommon and Reade's *Griffith Gaunt* (3 vols., 1866) so rare? All these novels were written at the height of their authors' reputation and published by firms of standing. Why are Mrs Gaskell's *Ruth* (3 vols., 1853) and Hardy's *The Trumpet Major* (3 vols., 1880), on the contrary, so much commoner than their position in their authors' literary career would suggest? Why does Cory's *Ionica* (1858), a book by an anonymous author of which only 500 copies were published at his own expense,[1] turn up at least as frequently as Browning's *Dramatis Personae* (1864), a regularly published product of one of the reigning poets of the day? But the multiplication of such mysteries is too mortifying to pursue further.

There must, of course, be reasons for the unexplained disparities in all these cases, as in dozens like them; probably a number of reasons and possibly complicated ones. It is simply that we are unable to bring to bear upon them a sufficient knowledge of the circumstances of original publication, the ups and downs of repute in which the books have from time to time been held, the tastes and habits of subsequent owners, and half a dozen other possibly relevant factors. Consequently, such observed results seem freakish: and perhaps more freakish to the experienced eye than to the novice. For beyond the many special likelihoods belonging to books of a certain period or a certain class, of a particular author or issued by a particular publisher, there are a few general probabilities inducible from accumulated experience. And if the study of comparative rarity is of fairly recent date, we can draw on a body of evidence left by earlier collectors, cataloguers and bibliographers which is none the less valuable because they themselves were not concerned to infer the general from the particular.

It is obvious that a big book on good paper survives better than a small one on poor paper, so that late Venetian *incunabula* are common and Savonarola's tracts are rare. It is less obvious, but no less true, that books, however big, that were printed for constant use, like collections of madrigals, surgical atlases or service books, will be worn out quicker than books, however small, printed for the gentleman's library. It is a commonplace that school books, grammars and children's or boys' books survive in tatters if at all: *Tom Brown's Schooldays* (1857) is among the rarest of nineteenth-century first editions in presentable shape, while no single copy is known to survive of the Sweynheim and Pannartz edition of

---

[1] Of the 500 only 311 had been sold by 1872; and if, as might be supposed, the author gave a larger number than usual away, the supposition has little evidential support, for presentation copies are of the utmost rarity.

Donatus's grammar (1464) or the original printing of *Goody Two Shoes* (1765) and only one of *Peter Parley* (1827). Exiguity makes for rarity, as in Dryden's *To my Lord Chancellor* (1662) or Sir Thomas Browne's *Letter to a Friend* (1690); and when added to a topical purpose, for great rarity, witness the early indulgences and almanacs, *The Drapier's Letters* (Dublin, 1724), the *Manifest der Kommunistischen Partei* (1848) or half a dozen of Shelley's political productions.[1] So, perhaps, does notoriety of a scandalous kind: the 'Antwerp' edition of Rochester's *Poems on Several Occasions* (actually London, 1680) and John Cleland's *Memoirs of a Woman of Pleasure*[2] (2 vols., 1749) would certainly support the theory, not to mention one or two of Swift's poetical pieces. It is *broadly* true that in relation to their original printing number plays have proved more perishable than fiction, fiction than poetry (except in the eighteenth century), poetry than essays, essays than biography or history, and anything than divinity (except perhaps law). Of books which were frequently revised, were reprinted in more elegant format or were included in a collected set, the original edition will have been discarded more often than of those not so dignified: on the other hand, books not reprinted but not utter failures, suffer from harder use. Books printed in out-of-the-way places are scarcer than those distributed from recognised centres, just as early books in vernacular languages are scarcer than their contemporaries printed in latin. Anonymity is a valid passport to the discard and pseudonymity (in an author commonly known by his own name) hardly less. Books which someone has troubled to bind in morocco will survive others in calf or sheep or cloth not only because morocco is more durable in itself but because it looks expensive; so that Rogers's *Italy* with Turner's plates (1830) will be saved when the Kilmarnock Burns (1786) goes to the pulping mill.

---

[1] E.g. *The Necessity of Atheism* (Worthing, 1811), *Proposals for a Society of Philanthropists* (Dublin, 1812), *Declaration of Rights* (Dublin, 1812), *The Devil's Walk* (1812), etc.

[2] Better known under her own name of Fanny Hill.

One could prolong such rash generalisations *ad infinitum*. It is perhaps more useful to try to isolate certain factors which, acting sometimes in combination, sometimes in opposition to each other, contribute to some sort of rationale of survival probability, or expectable rarity, against which a particular book may be assessed.

We must first of all recognise one overriding consideration: that the earlier the date of the book the greater will normally be the number of unknown quantities in its equation. We know more about the contemporary reputations of nineteenth- and twentieth-century authors than of sixteenth or seventeenth, more about later book-production and distribution than about earlier, more about the habits of nineteenth-century bibliophiles than Hanoverian or Caroline. The ledgers of Macmillan and Bentley survive, but those of Herringman and Gilliver are dust. Even the exceptions prove the rule, whether the tidy records of Strawberry Hill or the patiently reconstructed mosaic which Shakespeare's publishers owe to a whole generation of minute research. It is therefore of necessity and not from any predilection that most of the examples now to be cited date from the eighteenth and nineteenth centuries; for all the factors they illustrate are more nearly valid, and some are only valid, for comparatively modern books.

We must also bear constantly in mind the subtraction from the original printing number of any book more than a few decades old which must be made before we reach the area where it can begin to be classified for practical purposes even as common, let alone scarce or rare. Quite apart from the great mass of unscanned books in uninterested ownership, effectively secluded from actual circulation, there is the much greater mass of books which have been, and every year continue to be, destroyed by fire, water or other hazards, discarded as waste paper or sent to the pulping-mills. Of the *Bay Psalm Book* 1700 copies were printed in 1640: 11 are recorded today. Of Gray's *Elegy* (1751) the first edition is believed to have comprised 1000 copies: do more than 50 survive? The extant copies of Trollope's first novel, *The MacDermots of Ballycloran* (3 vols., 1847) could be numbered on three hands, perhaps on two. Yet 400 were printed only a hundred years ago. These are acknowledged rarities. But if we take a recent book and one admittedly 'common' by collecting standards, we must recognise the same principle, even if our estimate of the number of surviving copies has to be based on guess-work. There were only 350 copies of *A Shropshire Lad* issued with the London 1896 title-page. During the fifteen or twenty years that the first edition has been widely sought after, an average of perhaps three copies a year have appeared in the market. If we double or even treble that to include the copies which a high price has not dislodged from reverent or disinterested shelves, we still have half the edition unaccounted for.

It is, in fact, probably safe to say that by comparison with its original printing almost any book of a moderate antiquity is likely to survive today in tenuous numbers. It is only by collectors' standards and in relation to a perhaps apathetic demand that it can properly be called common. It is right that the word *rare* should be used with the utmost circumspection by collectors and the trade; but it is useful also to remember that our standard is, as it should be, a thing apart.

We must further remember that peculiarities or shortcomings in the physical make-up of a book may affect its chances of survival, and still more its chances of survival in good, if not fine, original condition. Many seventeenth-century books were printed on miserable paper, so that after no great use or lapse of time they would look fit only for the waste-basket and too often achieve it. The same handicap applies to a good many plays of the eighteenth century—*The School for Scandal* (Dublin, 1780) is a well-known example. With the nineteenth century, the trouble is more often in the covers: whether because a book was bound by the gutta-percha process, like Plimsoll's *An Appeal for Seamen* (1873) and a number of the illustrated books of the sixties, or wire-stapled, like Trollope's *The Duke's Children* (3 vols., 1880), and therefore falls apart; or because the fabric used was friable, so that the joints split, as is usually the case with *Shirley* (3 vols., 1849) and Melville's *The Whale* (3 vols., 1851); or simply because the dye in the cloth proved to fade easily, as in *In Memoriam* (1850), *Cranford* (1853) and *The Woman in White* (3 vols., 1860), so that really bright copies are almost never seen. In some more modern books the substitution of coloured ink or applied paint for the conventional gilding produced lettering which has proved almost invariably evanescent: familiar examples are Erskine Childers' *The Riddle of the Sands* (1903), R. Austin Freeman's *The Red Thumb Mark* (1907) and *The Old Wives' Tale* (1909).

With these general considerations in mind, then, let us proceed. The principal factors to be taken into account in assessing the comparative rarity of books are, by my count, eight in number, and they are as follows:

   (i) The number printed.
   (ii) Limited editions and the connoisseur's market.
   (iii) The book's subsequent repute, and thence its chances of preservation.
   (iv) The stability and efficiency of the publisher and the width of the original distribution.
   (v) Over-printing and 'remainders'.
   (vi) Rarity in collector's state v. rarity in any state.
   (vii) The position of the book in its author's literary career.
   (viii) Traditional or fallacious rarity.

The first of these factors is the number printed, which, if it can seldom be precisely ascertained, can sometimes be approximately hazarded from contemporary practice. The original printing of *Paradise Lost* (1667) was probably 1300 copies and the size of the edition (which took three years to sell out), combined with its substantial format, explains why the book is comparatively common today. The original printing of Fielding's *Amelia* (4 vols., 1752), coming after the great success of *Tom Jones* (6 vols., 1749), was (we also happen to know)[1] 5000, a very large number for an eighteenth-century novel. Other things being equal, therefore, it is not surprising that it is four or five times commoner today than the same author's *Joseph Andrews* (2 vols., 1742), of which only

[1] From the Strahan ledgers, piously preserved by Messrs Spottiswoode, Ballantyne and Co.

1500 had been printed ten years earlier. Of Boswell's *Johnson* (1791) 1750 were printed, in two volumes quarto—a big edition for a book of this kind, but publisher as well as author had reason to expect a best-seller. Of the success of Gibbon's *Decline and Fall* (1776–88), however, also in quarto, the promoters were less sanguine; and as the decision to increase the number for the first volume from 500 to 1000 was taken after a large part of the book was printed off, only 500 sets of the six volumes were first editions throughout.[1] If other things were equal, Boswell should be three or four times commoner today than a set of Gibbon with the first volume correct. In fact, since Boswell has been longer regarded by collectors and since among laymen needing house-room six volumes quarto will sometimes be jettisoned when two might be reprieved, the ratio is a good deal steeper.

With books of more modern date the number originally printed is increasingly overshadowed in importance by other considerations. Charles Reade's *Christie Johnstone*, published by Bentley in 1853, is a fairly common book. Edward Creasy's *Fifteen Decisive Battles of the World* (2 vols.), published by the same firm in 1851, is a very rare book indeed. Yet 500 were printed of each. The first edition of Darwin's *Origin of Species* (Murray, 1859) was 1250 copies; but it is far from rare today. Green's *Short History of the English People* (1874), on the other hand, is a notably difficult book to find: yet Macmillan's original printing was 3000. But if other factors are dominant here, and in a thousand similar cases, the number printed must always have some influence: Doughty's *Travels in Arabia Deserta* (2 vols., Cambridge, 1888) can never be very common, for only 500 were done. And Galsworthy's *Swan Song*, published forty years later, can never be really rare, for its first printing was 45,000.

The second factor is a special extension, or rather a modification, of the first. Books which were deliberately printed in small numbers or for a collector's market will have been, at the moment of issue, rarer than those printed for regular commercial distribution.

[1] J. E. Norton, *Bibliography of Gibbon* (1940), p. 38.

But whether their limitation was allied to a fine format or was due to the author's wanting something special to give to his friends, they are far more likely than the generality to have been solicitously treated by their original purchasers or recipients and preserved, even if not treasured, by subsequent owners. It is probable that 95 per cent of every edition put out from the Kelmscott Press is carefully shelved somewhere today, whereas it is doubtful whether 5 per cent survive of such contemporaries as *The Dolly Dialogues* (1894) or *Dodo* (2 vols., 1893). Similarly Trollope's *How the Mastiffs Went to Iceland* (1878), a privately printed souvenir of a yachting cruise, will be found more frequently than *Is He Popenjoy?* (3 vols.), a novel which was published in the same year under ordinary commercial conditions; and much more frequently in good condition. And the same argument holds good, though perhaps rather less forcibly, for copies of any book, of any date, which bear a presentation inscription from the author: for that which was precious to the original recipient and may in due time throw some devout collector into an ecstasy is likely to command at least the lip-service of retention from intervening owners. It would be premature to state dogmatically that presentation copies of the first edition of *East Lynne* (3 vols., 1861) are commoner than shabby or rebound copies. But it is a fact that well-preserved examples in the author's specially gilded presentation binding, of which twelve were done, have proved up to date less desperately rare than fine copies of the regular issue. For they were better cared for. Similarly Meredith's *Poems* (1851) survives, and often in fair order, more freely than its small circulation would otherwise render likely, because the author gave a large proportion of the edition away; and as for Talfourd's *Ion* (1836), an ordinary copy was once catalogued by a realistic book-seller with the note 'of the greatest rarity uninscribed'.

The third factor, which is as important as it is often difficult to assess, is the effect exerted on the survival probability of a book by the esteem in which it has been held by collectors, as distinct from mere unconscious owners, in previous times; and on its condition, if it does survive, by their bibliophilic habits. We have considered, in the first part of this book, some of the recent changes in taste and technique which have affected not only what has been preserved but the manner of its preservation; and we are to consider in the next chapter the whole question of 'condition'. We will therefore simply note here that the longer a book has been cherished by collectors, the greater its chances of occurrence today. Baskerville's books were produced for connoisseurs and, though collected with varying intensity during the past century, they have always commanded respect. Except, therefore, for ephemera (such as type-specimens) and certain marginal publications (such as Berners's *Treatyse of Fysshyng with an angle*, printed as late as 1827 with Baskerville types), they are naturally commoner, *edition for edition*, than the issues of Dodsley or Donaldson. Moreover, since they were mostly dignified by a superior binding, they are commoner in good condition. Mr Hazen has observed[1] that the elegant illustrated reprint of *The Castle of Otranto* produced in 1791 by Bodoni for one London publisher is a common book today, although only 300 were printed; while an inconspicuous commercial edition issued in the same year by another London publisher is extremely rare, though the printing was probably larger. For no one has troubled to preserve it. The products of the Aldine Press, though the Penguins of their day and designed specifically for the pocket, not the cabinet, were, later, extensively and keenly collected for many years. Consequently, though they have been out of fashion, simply *as* Aldines, for half a century now, most of them are still common enough; and such is the power of tradition that though the booksellers price them in accordance with current taste, they will not wittingly consign them to the salvage bin. And the same is true of Elzevirs. Again, books illustrated by Thomas Bewick were highly regarded—and therefore well bound and cared for—by his contemporaries and by several succeeding generations. They then fell into a profound doldrum. Yet their recent and deserved revival among specialists finds the market well supplied, for the substratum was intact.

The reverse side of the medal is of course much more striking:

[1] *A Bibliography of Horace Walpole*, New Haven, 1948.

those whole categories of books which owe their rarity today to their disregard, not necessarily by their original readers, but by subsequent generations. It is true that many spectacular examples of this are supplied by early English literature, so that the mere passage of time is often considered reason enough for the almost complete disappearance of some of the original editions of Howard or Marlowe or Shakespeare. In fact, however, a more effective cause is the length of time during which such books were disregarded. The longer and more absolute the neglect, the scarcer the book. Though the passage of two or three centuries gravely intensifies the effect, a formidable degree of rarity can be achieved in a much shorter time by a thoroughly neglected book, as anyone who collects guide-books, Wisbech imprints or early yellow-backs will bear witness.

Unregarded books get steadily scarcer every year, since the normal process of consumption and attrition is not offset by any preservative measures. But once a book achieves some measure of esteem, however limited, that process is to a proportionate extent arrested. It cannot become any less rare in an absolute sense, since only so many copies remain in existence: but it is likely to become commoner of occurrence, since copies will be brought to light by the demand of collectors. It ceases to lose ground as soon as it becomes an object of respect.

Fourthly, there is the stability, efficiency and interest of the book's publisher, on which depended its original start in the world. This factor increases in importance with the development of publishing as an independent trade, becoming almost paramount in respect of nineteenth- and twentieth-century books. As I cannot improve on its exposition by Mr Sadleir in his *Trollope: A Biblio-graphy*, the classic study of the principles of comparative rarity as applied to a richly complicated author, I shall quote his proposi-tions,[1] even though I refer you to the source for his argument. They are three, and they are as follows:

'(i) It will generally be found that books issued over an obscure or financially uncertain imprint have made rarer first editions than

[1] Pp. 252, 253.

those from big and well-established houses. This tendency is independent of the book's original printing numbers.'

If the Brontë sisters' *Poems* (1846), of which Aylott and Jones were stated (by the authors) to have sold only two copies, is the classic example, Mayne Reid collectors have learned to curse the names of Skeet and Shoberl, the mavericks who published his two earliest novels. It would be tedious to multiply examples and a handful will suffice. Captain Marryat's *Newton Forster* (3 vols., James Cochrane, 1832), William Barnes' *Poems of Rural Life* (John Russell Smith, 1844), Rolf Boldrewood's *Robbery under Arms* (3 vols., Remington, 1888), Conan Doyle's *The Sign of Four* (Spencer Blackett, 1890), and Katherine Mansfield's *In a German Pension* (Stephen Swift, 1911) are all books which owe their rarity today in large part to the instability of their original publishers.

'(ii) If an author has been to one house for the majority of his books, but has, here and there, arranged for an isolated work to be published by some other firm, the books issued by his regular publisher will, in the main, be more accessible to a collector fifty years afterwards than will be those bearing an exceptional imprint.'

All Meredith's novels before 1880 are scarce: but the scarcest is *Rhoda Fleming* (3 vols., 1865), his solitary aberration from his two regulars, Smith Elder and Chapman and Hall, to Tinsley; while *Romola* (3 vols., 1863), the only George Eliot novel not published by Blackwood, occupies a similar position in her table of comparative rarities.

'(iii) A book of one class published by a firm not known for that particular *genre* of work is liable to become a rarity, however well-established and renowned that firm in its own special line.'

Newman's two novels, *Loss and Gain* (1853) and *Callista* (1856), both issued by religious publishers, are cases in point, as is Wilkie Collins's *Man and Wife* (3 vols., 1870). For some inscrutable reason this was issued through F. S. Ellis, the antiquarian and Pre-Raphaelite publisher, whose imprint is not known on any other novel; and it is today the rarest title in its author's whole bibliography.

The fifth factor is a sort of rider, almost a caveat, to the fourth. For whereas, in general, wide distribution of a book makes for survival, though not necessarily survival in fine original state, there are cases where a number of copies of an unsuccessful book, instead of being pulped, have been preserved intact. We must be wary, therefore, of books originally published in an ordinary commercial manner, of which many very fine and very few normally battered copies are to be found. There may be a fishy reason behind the apparent paradox, and, if so, though their fineness is no whit abated by frequency, it must be denied the attribute of rarity and estimated (in price) accordingly.

A well-known example is Melville's *Mardi*, published in 1849 by Harper and Brothers of New York. The author's first two books *Typee* (1846) and *Omoo* (1847) had been very popular, and his publishers, naturally hoping for a big sale for the third, apparently printed a large edition. But the book was a dismal failure; as a result it is today easily the commonest of all Melville's first editions.[1] Two English novels of the same period well illustrate the effect of publishing circumstances on subsequent rarity. The first edition of Dickens's *Great Expectations*, published in three volumes by Chapman and Hall in 1861, is a rare book: Thackeray's *The Adventures of Philip*, published in three volumes by Smith Elder in the following year, is a common book. The former had been serialised in its author's magazine *All the Year Round*, the latter in its publisher's magazine *The Cornhill*. Both authors were famous, both publishers eminent. Why the disparity? The answer is that Dickens and his publishers, having had a failure with the issue in serial parts of *A Tale of Two Cities* (1859), decided to desert the normal (for Dickens) part-issue for publication in three-decker form.[2] Their hesitation was reflected in their handling of the probably not very large printing; for when the small first binding-up was exhausted, they furnished later ones (still of the same sheets) with title-pages which disingenuously but encouragingly proclaimed them new editions. There were five or more of these 'editions' (bibliographically, issues) within the year, and the rarity

---

[1] Richard Curle, op. cit., pp. 129, 130.
[2] John C. Eckel, *The First Editions of Charles Dickens* (1932), p. 91.

of the first is therefore due more to a promotional artifice than to the book's popularity, even if the latter did exceed the publisher's none too great expectations. Of *Philip*, on the other hand, we know[1] that 1520 copies were printed, of which 1100 were bound up before the end of the year. But Thackeray's powers were failing and the book did not live up to even this modest estimate. It never achieved an individual reprint and a 'remainder' of over 300 copies was sold off (in quires) in 1878. In this case the combination of overprinting and unpopularity gives us the same result as with *Mardi*; and since the libraries had little use for the book, while Thackeray's admirers loyally bought copies, the numerous survivors are mostly in good condition.[2]

More specialised in origin, but similar in their results, are those cases where a bundle of copies of some book have turned up years after it has reached, through a steady collectors' demand over a period, a fairly stable assessment of scarcity: a circumstance which immediately nullifies that assessment. A well-known example is the Strawberry Hill edition of Gray's *Odes* (1757), of which a small stock, in fine original condition, was discovered about thirty years ago (probably survivors of the 35 sold off in lots in 1810).[3] This exaggerated the commonness of a never uncommon book until Mr Hazen's disclosure in 1942 of the existence and nature of Kirgate's reprint, whence these copies undoubtedly derived. Similar (but authentic) 'delayed remainders' have been noted of Shelley's *Laon and Cythna* (1818), Bulwer Lytton's *Ismael* (1820) and *Weeds and Wildflowers* (1826), Peacock's *Rhododaphne* (1818), *The Misfortunes of Elphin* (1829) and *Crotchet Castle* (1831), Christina Rossetti's *Verses* (1847), Tennyson's *A Welcome* (1863), E. B. and R. Browning's *Two Poems* (1854) and other collected books; and no doubt many more have occurred unnoticed, to mystify contemporary observers and confound the historian.

[1] From the Smith Elder records, by courtesy of Messrs John Murray. For the details see Carter, *Binding Variants* (1932), p. 158.
[2] I have excluded the possibility that the 'remainder' was put up in the original style because, though I suspect it, it has not been proved.
[3] A. T. Hazen, *A Bibliography of the Strawberry Hill Press* (1942), p. 28.

The sixth factor in explaining or forecasting comparative rarities leads logically from its predecessors and again is chiefly applicable to nineteenth- and twentieth-century books. This is the distinction between books which are uncommon in any condition and books which may be common enough tattered or rebound but are rare in good original state. We have seen that a creditable start in the world and wide distribution make for survival. But contemporary popularity is destructive of the outward gloss. And if this is true of all books, it is particularly true of English novels from 1800 to 1890, which, in the dominant three-decker format, were more often borrowed from the circulating library than bought and kept. As for the exceptions, those potential best-sellers issued in serial parts for purchase on the instalment plan, they will obviously be common books because the editions were so large. It is equally obvious that copies rebound in half leather or put up in the publishers' cloth cases [1] will be in the majority and sets of the flimsy paper-covered parts in the small minority. [2]

Yet even here a further qualification is necessary. For though mediocre copies of part-issued novels in their cloth-bound form are in general commoner than sets of the same books in parts, really fine copies are by no means always so. If Thackeray, Lever and Ainsworth demy octavos are fairly often seen in good order, some of Surtees and Trollope are very seldom to be found so, and many of Dickens hardly ever. The cloth cases provided for his usually ample volumes were of poor quality, so that the collector may find *Martin Chuzzlewit* (1844) and *David Copperfield* (1850) as difficult, and *Pickwick* (1837) more difficult, to secure in fine original cloth than in the parts.

Ninety per cent of English fiction during this period, however, conformed (for its first publication in book form) to the three, or more rarely two, volume format, depending heavily on the lending libraries for its distribution: and the library is the graveyard of fine

---

[1] For some discussion of this practice see the present writer's *Binding Variants*, p. 74.

[2] There are one or two exceptions to this. Dickens's *Edwin Drood* (1870), for instance, is possibly commoner in parts than in the publisher's cloth: for it was over-printed, and sets of the original numbers could still be obtained from Chapman and Hall's trade counter well into the present century.

original condition. Consequently, although 'copy for copy' (i.e. regardless of condition) Victorian novels are in general commoner today than eighteenth-century novels, they are mostly very uncommon indeed in really well-preserved state; and it is harder to find *Henry Esmond* (3 vols.), which was published in 1852, in fine original cloth than a fine copy in its original calf of *Amelia* (4 vols.), which was published exactly a century earlier. Poetry is less affected during the age of cloth: and though they were both successfully published in 1868, *The Moonstone* (3 vols.) is today very rare in fine state and uncommon even shabby or rebound, while *The Ring and the Book* (4 vols.) is common enough and usually in good condition, for it was bought not borrowed and it is a solidly made book. But in the age of boards, when rebinding rather than library labels was the hazard, neither department has any particular advantage. If there is not much to choose for scarcity between *Waverley* (3 vols., Edinburgh, 1814) and *Adonais* (Pisa, 1821) 'copy for copy', *Waverley* in boards is rarer than *Adonais* in wrappers. But Tennyson's *Poems* (2 vols., 1842) and Disraeli's *Coningsby* (3 vols., 1844) are about equally common in half leather and about equally rare—and that is, very rare—in fine original state.

The seventh factor is the position of the particular book in its author's literary career. In its simplest form this is familiar in the all-too-crude axiom that an author's first book will be his rarest. Donne's *First Anniversarie* (1611), Milton's *Comus* (1637), Congreve's *Incognita* (1692), Crabbe's *Inebriety* (Ipswich, 1775), Fanny Burney's *Evelina* (3 vols., 1778), Browning's *Pauline* (1833), Le Fanu's *The Cock and Anchor* (3 vols., Dublin, 1845) and a dozen other examples come readily to mind in support of this assumption. Yet the first books of Johnson and Gibbon, of Shelley, Tennyson and Swinburne, of Melville, Maugham and Ernest Hemingway, are by no means the rarest in their bibliographies. Broadly, however, it is true to say that an author's first book is unlikely to be common: for even if it was published by a substantial firm, which it often will not have been, its printing number will probably have been small and its distribution, unless it had a great success, spasmodic. But just as we have seen that at a later stage in an established author's career an unsuccessful book following a popular one may be overprinted, or a successful book following a failure underprinted, so also it sometimes happens, whether from dwindling popularity or a change of publisher or some distributional cause, that an author's late books are among the hardest to find fifty or a hundred years later, as collectors of Ainsworth, Wilkie Collins and even Trollope can bear witness. Nor can Factor Seven always be disentangled from Factor Four (the stability and efficiency of the sponsor), for the publisher is always a primary component in any combination of causes.

It may, indeed, be convenient at this point to illustrate the combined influence of the factors so far distinguished on the output of a single author. And George Eliot provides us with a representative and fairly well documented example. Her first book, *Scenes of Clerical Life*, was published in two volumes by Blackwood of Edinburgh in 1858. The author was already known to a small, rather highbrow public and the book had a small, rather highbrow success. Although Mudie, under considerable pressure, took a third of the copies, it was not 'library fiction' in the usual sense, and its distribution was mainly through purchase by thoughtful people. It is today a scarce book, for the edition[1] was a modest one (1000). But it is not rare, for it was not devoured by library subscribers. On the contrary, it sold slowly; and since it was not the kind of book to be much thumbed even by buyers, a far higher proportion of survivors are in presentable shape than they would have been if it had been popular.

[1] Most of these details are drawn from Cross's *Life*; but others, from the Blackwood records, I owe to Mr Sadleir, who is treating the whole subject of comparative rarities in Victorian fiction at some length in the forthcoming catalogue of his library, and to Mr Gordon S. Haight of Yale, who kindly opened to me his store of detailed knowledge of George Eliot's literary career.

The exact contrary is the case with *Adam Bede* (3 vols., 1859). Blackwood's printing number (2000)[1] was twice as large, being based on sanguine expectations as well as the performance of its predecessor: but the book was a far greater success than he had reckoned and the first edition sold out in two months. In addition, therefore, to the repeated demands of the libraries, purchased copies got a much harder reading, with the result that *Adam Bede* today, while being copy for copy somewhat commoner than *Scenes from Clerical Life*, is in fine state very much rarer.

With *The Mill on the Floss* (3 vols., 1860) Blackwood naturally increased his printing, to the substantial number of 4000. Even this proved barely enough to satisfy George Eliot's widening circle of actual purchasers as well as the now fully mobilised libraries, so that a reprint of 2000 was ordered shortly after publication. But it matched demand much more nearly, and in consequence copies of the book in nice condition are not uncommon today. *Silas Marner* (1861) was again printed in a large edition—5500 were subscribed before publication. But it was in one volume, and the libraries never liked one-volume novels. Nor did it increase its author's reading public. So, whether or not one is right in suspecting that a remainder of the original edition was disposed of when it later (1868) came to be reprinted at a cheaper price, it is not rare and is as often as not found in fine condition.

In 1863 Smith Elder paid George Eliot £7000[2] for the *Cornhill* serial rights plus the book rights for six years of *Romola*, which was published by them in three volumes in 1863. The story was not popular as a serial and the book was apparently printed in a conservative number. *Romola* is in consequence (and conformably to Sadleir's Proposition II) an uncommon book today in any condition, and very uncommon fine. With *Felix Holt* (3 vols., 1866) George Eliot returned to Blackwood, who, having paid £5000 for the book, overprinted heavily (5000 copies) for a tepid

[1] In all these cases I have given the round figures, excluding 'overs' printed to cover imperfections and review copies. The actual numbers printed of *Scenes* and *Adam Bede*, for instance, were 1050 and 2100.

[2] They had originally offered £10,000, but with conditions which the author would not accept.

reception and eventually 'remaindered' a substantial block of the edition to W. H. Smith's[1] library. It is not surprising therefore that the book is the commonest, whether in fine or foul condition, of all its author's novels.

With *Middlemarch* (1871–2) and again with *Daniel Deronda* (1876) Blackwood was persuaded by G. H. Lewes to try an ingenious method of tapping the part-issue market as well as the libraries, with a sort of hybrid—eight small stout octavo monthly parts at 5s. each, followed by four cloth volumes at two guineas the set. The vogue for shilling illustrated part-issues was over, and Blackwood was excusably doubtful of a compromise which might well have failed to please library borrowers without attracting instalment buyers. But in the event it was successful. Of *Middlemarch* over 4000[2] sets and of *Daniel Deronda* nearly 6000 were sold of the part-issues; while the libraries apparently bought in quires (1153 and 1630 sets respectively were sold thus) and did their own binding.[3] After these substantial sales, the expectations for the four-volume cloth-bound form of both books were naturally very conservative. Only 366 sets of *Middlemarch* and only 348 sets of *Daniel Deronda* were so issued, and this accounts for their scarcity today.[4] They are both rarer in fine state than *Scenes of Clerical Life* though possibly hardly so rare as *Adam Bede*; and *Deronda* is slightly the rarer of the two. The part-issues of both books (again expectably) are fairly common, but those of *Middlemarch* are very seldom found fine.

[1] Sadleir, *The Evolution of Publishers' Binding Styles* (1930), p. 95.

[2] The first printing of Part I was 2500. This was followed, before November 1871 was out, by a reprint of 1575, another of 1575 in December and a third of 1050 in January 1872. The first printing of Part II, in January, was 4200, followed immediately by a reprint of 1050. And all the following parts were printed in editions of 5250.

[3] 8-volume bindings on *Middlemarch* have not, I believe, been confidently identified. But sets of *Deronda* are familiar in a plain chocolate-maroon cloth, with commonplace gilt lettering.

[4] Examples have been noted of 4-volume cloth sets of *Middlemarch* which were clearly cased up from the parts; and it must be presumed that Blackwood conformed to the established practice of supplying cases to part-issue subscribers on request.

My eighth and final factor should perhaps qualify rather as a practical footnote, except that it does affect, however indirectly, the future survival probabilities of the books to which it currently applies. This is what may be called traditional rarity: a reputation based either on a genuine earlier condition now no longer obtaining or on a *dictum* by some revered authority or on a fallacious deduction from some fact, accurately or inaccurately recorded, in the book's early history.

Since cataloguers copy from other cataloguers—and not only booksellers' and auctioneers' cataloguers, either—a reputation for rarity sometimes clings to a book year after year in the face of all evidence to the contrary. For example, Hawthorne's *Fanshawe* (Boston, 1828) is generally considered a great rarity. Being his first book, it might be expected to be, and no doubt, in the days before American first editions were so much sought after, it was. But it has appeared thirty-seven times at auction alone in the fifty years of *American Book-Prices Current*;[1] and even allowing for resales of the same copy, against which must be set the unknown volume of private turnover, no book which occurs so frequently can justly be called very rare. Plenty of similar cases will occur to experienced collectors in almost any field. Gissing's *Workers in the Dawn* (3 vols., 1880), Arnold's *Alaric at Rome* (Rugby, 1840),[2] Bentham's *Fragment on Government* (1776), Byron's *Childe Harold* (4to, 1812), Coleridge's *The Fall of Robespierre* (1794), Blackmore's *Lorna Doone* (3 vols., 1869), Swinburne's *Atalanta in Calydon* (1865) and *The Devil's Due* (1875), Burton's *Anatomy of Melancholy* (Oxford, 1621), Johnson's *Rasselas* (2 vols., 1759), Kipling's *Letters of Marque* (Allahabad, 1891), Landor's *Poems from the Arabic and Persian* (1800)—to take a mere handful at random, are all books which, in different degrees (and none of them in the *Fanshawe* class), enjoy a reputation for rarity considerably in excess of their just deserts.

A good example of the influence of the authoritative statement is cited by Mr Richard Curle, who points out[3] that 'because

---

[1] Colton Storm, *A Half Century of Rare Book Prices* (1946).
[2] The original edition is at present commoner of occurrence than the Wise forgery.   [3] Op. cit., p. 105.

Mr Wakeman [the greatest collector of his day in this field] left in his leather-bound copy of Whittier's *Poems* (1838) a note saying "This book in original stamped morocco, gilt edges, is very rare. I have never seen another copy," it has been assumed ever since, and loudly proclaimed, that such is the case. But such is *not* the case. The book is not at all rare in morocco binding, and it is by mere chance that a dozen copies did not come into Mr Wakeman's hands.' Similarly it was sufficient for Wise[1] to state that 'in some early copies' of the first edition of *In Memoriam* two misprints occur, 'which were corrected in later copies', for the former to assume, and retain, the description of *the rare first issue*; whereas it is in fact those copies in which the two words have been corrected that are so rare that many Tennyson experts have doubted their existence. The same authority's elevation[2] of the 'uncancelled' state of leaf G1 in *Lyrical Ballads* (1798) to a position of desirability and presumptive rarity was adopted and embroidered by cataloguers for several decades despite constant evidence of its commonness. The delusion indeed may occasionally[3] still be met with, even after Professor George Whicher's demonstration[4] in 1937 that the leaf in question was never cancelled at all—at least, not by Wordsworth or his publisher.

As for the fallacious deduction, its most familiar form is the asseveration of rarity allegedly caused by the early withdrawal or suppression of a book, whether true or legendary. Often, of course, this does result in a book becoming rare. Collins's *Odes* (1747) is such a case, though it is ten times commoner than Gray's *Ode on a Distant Prospect of Eton College*, which, published in the same year, was never suppressed. If Beckford's *Dreams, Waking Thoughts and Incidents* (1783), a notorious rarity, is out of court as having never been actually issued, Landor's *Poems* (1795) and Byron's *Fugitive Pieces* (Newark, 1806) are examples of books suppressed by their authors and really rare today. But are they rarer than *Fourteen Sonnets* (Bath, 1789) by William Lisle Bowles, the poems whose

---

[1] *Ashley Catalogue*, vol. VII, p. 117.
[2] *Ashley Catalogue*, vol. VIII, p. 4.
[3] E.g. *Book-Auction Records*, 1943–4 (1946), p. 526.
[4] *The Colophon* (New Series, vol. II, no. 3).

'meliorating' effect on his own style was acknowledged by Southey but on which, unlike the latter's *Poems* (Bristol, 1797), the author laid no violent hands? or than Darley's *Nepenthe* (c. 1839)? or than the *Posthumous Fragments of Margaret Nicholson* (Oxford, 1810)? The 1865 edition of *Alice's Adventures in Wonderland* was rigorously suppressed, even if it was properly 'published' at all. It is certainly very rare: but it cannot compare with Edward Lear's *Book of Nonsense* (1846), of which not a single indisputably perfect copy in original state seems to be known today.

Yet if some such suppressions do produce genuine cases of subsequent rarity, others manifestly do not. For example, Galileo's *Dialogo sopre i due massimi Sistemi del Mondo* (Florence, 1632) is commonly stated to have been burned by the Inquisition. If this is true, it belies the reputation for efficiency which the Holy Office has for centuries enjoyed, for the book is far from rare today. A vague tradition used to exist that Beckford managed to suppress Henley's translation of *Vathek* (1786), the publication of which was unauthorised; and so for years a spurious rarity was attributed to what would now be recognised as one of the commoner first editions of the period. Of Matthew Arnold's *The Strayed Reveller* (1849), Richard Garnett, in *DNB*, recording that 500 only were printed, states further that 'it was withdrawn before many copies were sold and is very scarce'. It is *not* very scarce, though on the evidence it ought to be; and so it may have been in 1909, when Garnett wrote, for Arnold was not then much sought after. Nor are Robert Bridges's *Poems* (1873), George Moore's *Flowers of Passion* (1878), Charles Morgan's *The Gunroom* (1919), nor half a dozen other books which their authors are understood to have tried to suppress.

Since collectors and dealers, and even custodians of rare books in institutional libraries, are hardly likely to depreciate the degree of rarity which tradition or their own experience attaches to a book they are describing, it is only by a long process of tacit withdrawal that it will be dethroned from an undeserved eminence. A good many books, therefore, will continue to be called rare even when a steady demand combined with persistent occurrence has proved that, for the time being at any rate, they are not so. At the other end of the scale, candidates for promotion—from *scarce* to *very scarce* to *rare* to *very rare* to *exceedingly rare*: from *uncommonly found in fine condition* to *virtually unprocurable in any state*; from *unknown to Prism* through *no copy sold at auction since 1917* to the dizzy heights of *not in GKW* or *unrecorded and apparently unique*—such candidates are continually appearing, sometimes supported by a very imposing fanfare of trumpets. The prudent collector will maintain a judicious, even on occasions a positively Missourian, scepticism of claims by other than trusted experts, and especially claims which seem to do violence to the sort of probabilities which we have been discussing. No matter how great his experience, 'every collector will find', in the words of the epigraph to this chapter, 'that some books are commoner than might reasonably be expected and some decidedly rarer'. But he should at least do his best to make sure that such expectations as he has are reasonably based.

CHAPTER XII

CONDITION

The condition of a book must be seen to be realised, and condition
more than anything else nowadays dictates value and will continue
to dictate it. MICHAEL SADLEIR

Better a few books in the best available condition than a thousand in
tatterdemalion. WINTERICH AND RANDALL

I would take an ex-library copy rather than none at all.
PERCY H. MUIR

THE condition of the copy has been a major factor in connoisseurship since the earliest days of book-collecting. Yet
the implications of the phrase 'in collector's state' and even
the exact meaning of the term 'fine copy' have been, and remain,
constantly responsive to changes in bibliophilic convention. Moreover, the individual judgment of the collector has at all times
modified his own acceptance of the prevailing habit, so that differences of taste in this particular were as noticeable among the
collections forming a hundred years ago as they are today. Fasti-
diousness varies in kind as well as in degree.

Burton,[1] for example, instructively compares the opposing attitudes of those two giants W. H. Miller and Richard Heber, to the
nowadays all-important question of the purity, as distinct from the
handsome appearance, of a book. The former's experience, he
wrote, 'aided by a heaven-born genius tending in that direction,
rendered him the most merciless detector of sophisticated[2] books.
Nothing, it might be supposed on first thought, can be a simpler
or more easily recognised thing than a book genuine as printed.
But in the old-book trade there are opportunities for the exercise
of ingenuity inferior only to those which render the picture-
dealer's and the horse-dealer's functions so mysteriously interesting.
Sometimes entire facsimiles are made of eminent volumes. More

[1] Op. cit., p. 25.
[2] This is the earliest use (1862) known to me of 'sophisticated', meaning
'doctored', applied to rare books.

171

commonly, however, the problem is to complete an imperfect copy. This will be most satisfactorily accomplished, of course, if another copy can be procured imperfect also, but not in the same parts. Great ingenuity is sometimes shown in completing a highly esteemed edition with fragments from one lightly esteemed....It will establish a broad distinction to note the fact, that whereas our friend the Archdeacon [i.e. Heber] would collect several imperfect copies of the same book in the hope of finding materials for one perfect one among them, Inchrule [i.e. Miller] would remorselessly spurn from him the most voluptuously got-up specimen (to use a favourite phrase of Dibdin's), were it tainted by the very faintest "restoration".'

This particular element of 'condition' is only one of several, though it is perhaps the most important one. And it will therefore be well to begin by distinguishing some others. For the description 'a fine copy' has not only meant different things at different times and to different people:[1] it can mean different things in different circumstances, even when accurately and scrupulously used. In its most absolute sense, I suppose, the term 'fine', applied to any book of any period, could be said to mean no more (if no less) than that all its leaves were present, clean, whole and amply margined; that it was sound and undisturbed in its binding; and that that binding, whatever its material, was fresh and unblemished and, if of leather, of a sufficient elegance to raise it above the modest category of 'neat'.

In this sense 'fine' would be equally applicable to a copy of the Jenson *Pliny* (Venice, 1472) in contemporary stamped vellum, to another in the sober but handsome morocco which Lewis or Hering would have put on it for Lord Vernon, or to a third bound by Douglas Cockerell for St John Hornby in oak boards with a pigskin back. It could be justly used of *The Castle of Otranto* (1765) in original wrappers, of another copy in original trade calf and of yet a third bound for some contemporary grandee in armorial red morocco. It would further be applicable to copies of *Barchester Towers* (3 vols., 1857), *Uncle Silas* (3 vols., 1864), *The Mayor of Casterbridge* (2 vols., 1886) and *Brideshead Revisited* (1945),

[1] For an eighteenth-century example see above, p. 120, note 1.

whether they were in their original cloth or in a glossy full levant morocco binding with gilt edges.

The layman might not see much to choose between the three copies of *Pliny*. He would certainly disdain the wrappered *Otranto*. He would probably be more impressed by the Zaehnsdorf or Sangorski and Sutcliffe copies of the novels than by those in commonplace cloth. But the collector assesses fine condition on a quite different and much stricter basis: first in terms of the bibliophilic conventions and secondly of his own taste. He recognises two further qualities, the 'original' and the 'appropriate'. He will certainly condemn the rebound modern novels as neither, and here convention is at its most rigorous. If the first *Pliny* possesses both qualities and therefore commands his preference, the others will probably possess the second and therefore his respect. With the *Otranto* he has a less regulated choice, first between three kinds of appropriateness and then between two kinds of originality, so that his own connoisseurship will be the arbiter within the limits of his purse.

The element of the 'appropriate' in the condition of a book must always be the most subjective and the least governable by bibliophilic rules. It also has more to do with the outside and less with the inside than the simple 'fine' or the often complex 'original'. The former of these qualities need not and the latter will not be present in a copy of Herbert's *The Temple* bound by the ladies of Little Gidding, or a volume of Coleridge covered for Southey in a bit of his favourite chintz. Yet both are appropriate in a most desirable degree. The three small volumes of *Sense and Sensibility* (1811) seem to some collectors more appropriate in the unassuming half leather and sprinkled edges in which Elizabeth Bennet might have borrowed them from Mr Hazard's lending library at Bath, than in either the originality of paper boards or the handsomest Bedford morocco, gilt tops, uncut—the official choices of today and yesterday respectively. Among *incunabula* and other early books the rebinding of the Roxburghe period has acquired in modern eyes a certain associative *patina* in addition to the mellowness of age and the physical qualities of dignified craftsmanship and generally appropriate design: so that the Milan *Lascaris* (1476), the Ratdolt *Euclid* (Venice, 1482) or the Florence *Homer* (1488) seem to us almost as much at home in a diced russia by Roger Payne or a morocco elegant by Kalthoeber as in the stamped leather or oak boards of their own century.

The tendency of collectors to rebind even dilapidated copies of earlier books has been curbed during the last fifty years by the increasing preference for original condition, however defective. Yet the practice is never likely to be entirely outmoded, since rebinding is often preferable to really drastic patching; and the style in which it is nowadays carried out is beginning to reflect the discrimination already applied by collectors to the more and the less appropriate rebindings of the past. The great binders of the late eighteenth and early nineteenth centuries took considerable pains to match cover to contents, and this tradition was maintained in the best work of their successors, particularly Bedford and Riviere. But even they, and some others more extensively, fell into a sort of formula for other than special jobs—a formula which seems to have satisfied most contemporary collectors. The result was that by the first quarter of the present century the same full-dress uniform of highly polished levant morocco or stained yellow calf, with fully gilt back, gilt edges and often gilt panelled sides as well, was imposed impartially on the great majority of those rare books, whether of 1470, 1670 or 1870, which a collector or a bookseller wished to rebind with any pomp and circumstance. It was, of course, the prevailing style and finish of the period, and its execution would often be the best of its kind. Such books were therefore being accorded the highest honours in contemporary protocol. Yet the results are sometimes as tasteless as the gothicising of a baroque church by a 'correct', careful and infinitely well-intentioned architect of the 1880's. In this matter English practice may have owed something, consciously or unconsciously, to the example of France, whose bibliophiles and binders have never allowed much variation from an iron rule. American practice certainly owed much, since French workmen supplied the *cadres* of several fashionable binderies.

This tedious uniformity was consciously opposed by such scholarly craftsmen as Cobden Sanderson and Douglas Cockerell, and there have always been exceptions among the output of the regular commercial shops, whether executed spontaneously or to the order of a strong-minded customer. In general, however, it is only within the past fifteen or twenty years that more than a handful of collectors and booksellers, more than an occasional binder, have looked objectively at the conventional, bright, gilt-splashed copies of *Volpone* (1607) or *The Way of the World* (1700), of Tom Paine's *Common Sense* (1776) or Byron's *Don Juan* (6 vols., 1819–24). Whether or not the knowledgeable collector of 1900 shared the *avant-garde* taste for original condition as a quality to be prized in its own right, he knew perfectly well that *The Faerie Queene* (2 vols., 1590–6) or *The Compleat Angler* (1653) would be more naturally clothed in plain calf, sheep or vellum, Johnson's *London* (1738) in marbled or plain grey wrappers or in quarter calf, than in the dress of his own day. But the conventions decreed a uniform grandeur rather than any appropriateness of style, and even today their hold is still strong. Yet it has been discovered by the discriminating, most of them collectors who revere original or contemporary condition but recognise that they cannot always get it, that a careful binder, carefully instructed, can produce[1] a quite acceptable modern version of the plain calf or vellum of 1650, the panelled calf or marbled boards and calf back of 1750. This style of rebinding, usually indicated by the qualification 'antique' in a bookseller's catalogue, is disliked by some as an archaistic imitation, inferior to an honest contemporary vernacular; and like all other aspects of the quality of appropriateness in a book, this will remain a matter of individual taste. I need not, therefore, conceal my own, which favours a binding in keeping both with the book's interior and with its genuinely original neighbours on the shelf. For your Florio's *Montaigne* (1603) or your *Tristram Shandy* (9 vols., 1760–7) in a shiny new morocco among the old calf of their contemporaries look to me like men in evening dress at an afternoon party.

[1] To speak strictly, he could in 1939 and one hopes he may again be able to in the nineteen fifties. He cannot in 1949.

If the 'appropriate' is a matter of taste, it might be thought that the 'original' is purely a matter of fact. Up to a point this is so. But such of the history of original binding before about 1825 as is known has not always been clearly interpreted either by collectors or the trade. And common sense has sometimes been wanting in the direction, as well as the sternness, with which the doctrine of original condition has been applied during the half century or so since it began to be generally accepted. We have seen that its importance for nineteenth-century books was successfully inculcated by the innovators of the nineties, while the same principles were being applied to early printed books by such collectors as George Dunn and C. S. Ascherson. It is now universally accepted for all books published after the date when publisher's binding standardised the appearance of the whole, or at least of a substantial part,[1] of the first edition of a book: a date somewhere between 1825 and 1830 for general books, but somewhat later for verse, because such books were usually slighter in bulk, and considerably later[2] for novels, owing to the complicated machinery of their distribution. For it is only of books produced after the publisher had assumed the responsibility for edition binding that it is possible to say with certainty (notwithstanding a few specialised exceptions) that a particular copy is or is not in the original binding as issued: and as issued, furthermore, not merely by the bookseller across the counter to his customer but, previously, by the publisher to the retailer. 'Original binding' is used by most collectors almost as an equivalent of 'publisher's binding'. This is inaccurate: but the narrowing of connotation is no doubt pragmatical; for it reflects the recognition, whether conscious or unconscious, that it is only when the original binding is identifiably a wholesale as well as a retail covering that the canonisation of copies in that condition can be demonstrably as well as theoretically sustained.

[1] For some discussion of variant and secondary bindings during the cloth period, see the present writer's *Binding Variants in English Publishing 1820–1900*.
[2] Novels were still being issued concurrently in full cloth, gilt, and in boards, cloth backs, paper labels, as late as the fifties.

I have stressed this point not from any personal preoccupation with publisher's cloth (notorious as this may be to my friends), but as an essential preliminary to our consideration of original condition in the period preceding standardisation of exterior— a period which extends all the way back from William Pickering, the first publisher to use cloth for edition binding, to Gutenberg himself. For if 'original binding' in its strictest sense means (as it does) no more than the undisturbed covering put on the book when first it was covered at all, it is surely incumbent on those devotees of the principle who collect books of the earlier centuries to be quite clear in their minds how they are going to define 'original', first for theoretical and then for practical purposes. Is it to mean:

(i) The binding original to the book, which shows no signs of having been preceded by earlier covers individual to it—that is, simply not a rebinding—even though it may not be demonstrably contemporary?[1]

(ii) Any binding demonstrably contemporary: whether judged to be so on stylistic grounds, which will sometimes be disputable, or from a dated original endpaper, which is as indisputable as it is unfortunately rare?

(iii) A binding which conforms closely enough in style to a number of others on the same book, or on similar books of the same date, to justify the presumption that it is a 'trade' binding?

(iv) Boards or wrappers, or the original stitching, innocent of either?

The first of these propositions offers far too much latitude to be approved by self-respecting collectors, and I do not think we need discuss it further. The last represents today's recognised ambition for later eighteenth- and early nineteenth-century books. The second, though perhaps it would be sensible to abandon 'original' for 'contemporary' as a description of such books, indicates the most favourable condition in which books before about 1740 can be expected to be secured by anyone and books before about 1810

---

[1] E.g. secondary or remainder publisher's bindings, bindings on books previously in wrappers or boards or extracted from a collected volume.

by most. The third, referring to what I have called 'trade binding', is the most controversial and perhaps the most interesting of them all: for, however difficult of application, it represents original condition *as issued for and to the public* and therefore offers the closest analogy to publisher's binding, which has been accepted as obligatory for books of later date.

It was perhaps natural that the fanatical followers of Wise, Forman and the other pioneer advocates of original condition for modern books should seek to push the boards-and-wrappers criterion, which was appropriate to the Romantic poets and not unreasonable for the Regency novelists, right back into the eighteenth century. The general adoption of publisher's cloth was slower in the keenly collected departments of verse and fiction than in any others; the impact upon them of edition binding was consequently not so decisive at the time nor its implications for collectors so obvious in retrospect; and it must have seemed natural enough to apply the same standards to Chatterton's *Rowley Poems* (1777) as to *Christabel* (1816) or *Liber Amoris* (1823), to *The Mysteries of Udolpho* (4 vols., 1794) as to *Quentin Durward* (3 vols., 1821) or *Peter Simple* (3 vols., 1834). But if it was natural, it was also in some respects unfortunate. For the idea took root that boards or wrappers represented the only genuinely original condition for any book of which a copy survived or might survive in such state, irrespective of publishing practice at the date of its issue. It was thus inevitable that a principle proper to the publisher's cloth period and plausible for the previous decade or two would be applied wholesale and absolutely to a period during which such a condition represented no more than an optional, and by intention ephemeral, alternative to the normal trade binding of leather or half leather. In the event, when the eighteenth century came into its own among collectors, it was so applied, and with a vengeance.

That the boards/wrappers convention for books earlier than about 1810 is still devoutly subscribed to is not due simply to the momentum of the pioneers and the misguided enthusiasm of the following generation. It is due partly to a genuine, if exaggerated, conception of the superiority of such copies over copies in original leather for bibliographical purposes, and partly to that preference for the certain over the disputable which is not peculiar to book-collectors. Among our four tentative definitions of original condition for pre-cloth books, only the last is not beset by uncertainties in practice. One copy of a boarded or wrapped book may, indeed often does, exhibit variations from other boarded or wrapped copies—variations which would set cloth-period collectors agog with visions of a primary or a secondary binding: but it clearly could not be more thoroughly original than it is. And that is the sheet-anchor. The collector who clings to it will sometimes admit that if a hundred copies of *Peregrine Pickle* (4 vols., 1751) were sold across the counter on publication day, all of them ready-bound in calf, no other, whether wrappered, boarded or in folded quires, could be more nearly in original state, *as issued*, than they: but he will reasonably ask how any one of them is to be positively identified.

He will also perhaps bring up the question of those untrimmed edges, by which we have been taught to set so much store. Now there is no doubt that, like really immaculate boards, a crisp deckle has a charm of its own, quite independent of the bibliographical propriety of full original measurements. Yet even here we have suffered from exaggeration. Collectors have at all times cherished, and rightly cherished, a good large copy of any book. But whereas a cloth-bound book is intended[1] to be a finished article and its type area is therefore accommodated to the margins provided, no book published before 1825 was expected, by those who produced and distributed it, or by those who bought it, to remain in its temporary envelope of wrappers or boards. On the contrary, it was expected to be bound, whether before sale in a trade binding, or after, to a customer's specification.[2] Consequently the page was

---

[1] Not quite from the earliest days, but from 1832 onwards certainly.

[2] By the end of the eighteenth century the gap between cheap readymade and expensive bespoke bindings was being bridged. James Lackington, the bookseller, referring to the early eighties, wrote (*Memoirs*, 1792 edition,

laid out (whether well or ill is irrelevant) with due allowance for the binder's shears. These were often ruthlessly applied, as we know; but that does not alter the fact that the much-prized deckle is no part of the finished product as it was seen in the mind's eye or on the counter of Tonson or Millar, of Baskerville or John Bell. We laugh good-humouredly at those collectors of the early nineteenth century who doted on a tall Elzevir and would pay five times as much for a copy with an extra eighth of an inch of height. But are we any less doting today?

There is ample documentation[1] for the regular sale of bound books across the counter at a specified price during the eighteenth and earlier centuries. (Thin poetical or dramatic pieces are an exception, for they were normally issued stitched and naked.) The fact that they were bound for the wholesaler or the retailer, not, as an entire edition, for the publisher, conforms to the practice of an earlier stage in the development of the publishing business and in no way affects their status. Such books fulfil every condition of originality of state as issued to the public; whereas copies in wrappers or boards, however bibliographically significant, however modishly seductive, are functionally nothing more than accidental survivors of the chrysalis stage in production, sold in semi-processed state for binding to the purchaser's individual taste. Yet collectors will probably continue to prefer the latter not merely until the theoretically unassailable status of original trade binding is more widely accepted, but further, until examples of it can be more confidently identified.

This is at present, and is likely to remain, a largely empirical business. Yet surely a sufficient number of moral certainties have been attained, by persistent observation and comparison based on the firm foundation of known practice, to convince anyone whose mind is open to circumstantial evidence, even if certain proof is

p. 362): 'My expenses were also exceedingly increased by the necessity I was under of keeping each article in a variety of different kinds of binding, to suit the various tastes of my customers.'

[1] For example, a newspaper advertisement of 28 February 1749 for *Tom Jones*: 'It being impossible to get sets bound fast enough to answer the demand for them, such gentlemen and ladies as please may have them sewed in blue paper and boards at the price of sixteen shillings a set.'

usually wanting. The approximate but striking uniformity of the
plain calf bindings, with numbered but unlettered backs, in which
so many copies of the novels of Fielding and Smollett (for instance)
are found, cannot be accidental. These are original trade bindings,
as are the limp vellum wrappers so commonly seen on the poetry
and divinity of the seventeenth century. It may perhaps be debated
whether those volumes of Keats and other Taylor and Hessey poets
which are often found in green or brown leather with an unmistakable strapwork design stamped on the sides are, or are not,
strictly trade or publisher's bindings; but few certainly would
withhold recognition from the standard panelled calf that covers
the majority of contemporarily bound copies of the 1726 and 1727
editions of *Gulliver's Travels*. In the last quarter of the eighteenth
century, the proprietary leather of John Bell has been conclusively
identified by Mr Morison[1] and Newbery's 'vellum manner' fully
documented by Mr Sadleir.[2] The experienced student of the books
of any author or category or decade between 1600 and 1800 could
easily add a dozen examples of indubitable trade bindings to this
handful, and any collector of seventeenth- or eighteenth-century
books could point to a score of specimens on his shelves.

But, alas, most of these cases can only be proved up to the hilt
by some happy accident like the original owner's date and price on
the endpaper. And in consequence acceptance of individual examples of trade bindings continues to be restricted to those collectors who have given the question enough attention to justify
confidence in their own and their fellow-experts' judgment. The
number of these is increasing: but the irrational supremacy of
boards and wrappers for the eighteenth century will be successfully
challenged only through a much wider recognition of the original
status of trade binding and a complementary narrowing of the
present gap in esteem between boarded copies and those in a
binding which, even if it cannot be established as 'trade', is at least
clearly contemporary. It is, indeed, in this direction that a return
to reason may most confidently be expected; for if the identification of trade binding necessarily calls for some degree of technical

[1] *John Bell* (Cambridge, 1930), pp. 113–15 and Pl. facing p. 115.
[2] *The Evolution of Publishers' Binding Styles*, p. 10 and Pl. I.

expertise, a just estimation of relative importance (rarity is another matter) between a boarded copy and another in contemporary leather is mostly a matter of common sense.

The consideration of the 'appropriate' and the 'original' as factors in the general question of condition has kept us looking mostly at the outside of the book. Even so we have left on one side, as being a special department, the collecting of bindings for their own sake; whether Groliers for beauty, armorials for historic interest, unusual designs for rarity or exotic materials for curiosity. Yet the criteria of condition applied to the interior of the book, if they are superficially simpler because they are more absolute, have yet differed considerably in different periods. They also differ not a little in any given period, according to the particular class of book to which they are applied.

We have said, speaking broadly, that the collector requires a book to be (a) complete, (b) clean and sound, and (c) undisturbed. But no collector progresses far without realising that he is often faced with copies in which he purchases the first or second of these qualities only at the expense of the third; and though his own judgment, here as elsewhere, will be his ultimate guide, he will find that bibliophilic custom accepts some compromises in these matters, while rejecting others. One book is complete because it has been made up from two imperfect copies. Another is clean because it has been washed. A third is sound in its covers because it has been recased or rejointed. Each of these may be a more satisfactory entity as the result of the attention it has received, but none of them qualifies as undisturbed. Moreover, none of them qualifies as honest unless the nature and extent of the disturbance, preferably accompanied by its date and the name of the executant, are clearly and indelibly recorded. And this is almost never done.

Burton's description of the divergent views of Heber and of W. H. Miller, which was quoted at the beginning of this chapter, is still apposite. The eighteenth-century practice, followed by Heber and many of his successors and not entirely discarded today, is nicely exemplified by a note written into one of his

books by that most scrupulous of collectors, Michael Wodhull.
It reads as follows:[1]

Ed.pr.	13	–
a 2nd copy	7	6
bind.	16	0
	1 16	6

After sorting the best leaves,
sold the 2nd copy at Leigh's
auction May 1797 for 8s. 6d.   8   6

Net.   1   8   –

Few today would be so lavish as to sacrifice two apparently
complete copies to make one superior one. The question is more
often one of what we have learned to call 'cannibalisation': the
perfecting of a damaged example from another or others hopelessly crippled. And its propriety is normally assessed according
to the rarity and antiquity of the book concerned. Just as incompleteness, which would be intolerable in *The Jungle Book* (1894) or
Treasure Island (1883), *The Beggar's Opera* (1728) or *All for Love*
(1678), is considered excusable in the Mainz *Psalter* (1457) or
Petrarch's *Sonnets* (Venice, 1470), *Euphues* (1578) or *The Countess
of Pembroke's Arcadia* (1590), so is 'making-up' overlooked in
books of outstanding rarity, age and importance. Messrs Winterich
and Randall[2] have well summed up the contemporary attitude.
'The substitution or insertion [they write] of a signature or a page
is in most cases frowned upon by the cognoscenti, and properly,
yet the grafting of wanting leaves from a hopelessly imperfect copy
has the sanction of long tradition, and is certainly as respectable
a procedure as the patching of a Tudor bedstead. But the book has
to be rare and costly to lend the procedure the dignity it has
acquired, and the fact of substitution must, of course, be proclaimed
and not concealed. And thereby what would be at worst a fraud
and at best a total destruction of sentimental and commercial
value in the instance of a *Scarlet Letter* or a *Raven* or a *Way of all
Flesh* becomes an accepted bibliophilic convention where a Caxton
or a Shakespeare folio or a *Pilgrim's Progress* is concerned. It all
sounds suspiciously like class legislation, and it is.'

[1] Quoted from Quaritch's *Dictionary of Book-Collectors*, part 9 (1897).
[2] Op. cit., p. 76.

To this general convention certain exceptions are admitted. For complexity of issue is sometimes accepted as a legitimate substitute for age and rarity in extenuation of the making-up of copies. The King James Bible of 1611, for example, is neither very old nor very rare, but thanks to its issue points, its special liability to incompleteness, and the wholesale ministrations of Francis Fry, who specialised in the book, most surviving copies are made up and are not disdained therefor. *She Stoops to Conquer* (1773) is rich in bibliographical complications, so is Irving's *Salmagundi* (1807-8), so, *par excellence*, is *Pickwick* (1836), and any collector who wants a copy with all the points prescribed by the bibliographers reconciles himself to accepting it made up, for probably hardly a single one was originally issued with every detail 'correct'.

The importance of blank leaves, inserted advertisements and other material marginal to completeness has been much debated.[1] The question of advertisements, in particular, provided a regular Aunt Sally for the bibliographers and commentators of the twenties and thirties. They were once extravagantly over-rated, and there was certainly need in 1930 for Mr Curle's emphatic statement[2] that 'we must keep vividly before us the fundamental irrelevance of inserted advertisements'. This and similar injunctions, buttressed by the manifestly tendentious antics of some of the enthusiasts, have had their effect, and it is probable that less concern for inserted advertisements is shown by careful collectors today than by those of thirty-five years ago. Nor has the passion for dust-jackets remained at the generally high pitch attained during the twenties, while the tendency to treat a previous owner's name on the fly-leaf as a blemish rather than a provenance is nowadays properly recognised as an illogical crotchet.[3]

The question of washing, repairing and recasing is a more complicated one. The need is normally less urgent than with making-up, since the one involves completing something positively imperfect, while the others merely improve something

[1] See above, p. 104.   [2] Op. cit., p. 16.
[3] Cf. Winterich and Randall, op. cit., p. 82.

dirty, dog-eared, battered or shaken. But since there is more occasion for them, these practices are certainly very much commoner; they are not by any means always avowed; and their results are sometimes very difficult to detect. The collector consults his own taste in deciding whether to leave one of his own books as it is or to have it repaired, and he commits no offence against bibliographical propriety if he decides for repair, for he knows precisely what was inside the covers before his binder took them off. But unless that collector recorded indelibly in the book the nature of the repairs made to it—and unfortunately very few do so [1]—it will in due course take its place on other shelves where, like its neighbours, it must be judged without benefit of any special knowledge. There, if the washing or recasing has been done tolerably well, the result will very possibly deceive the novice, which is neither desirable in itself nor was desired by the original owner. But only the most expert and expensive doctoring will deceive a veteran collector or a dealer. Washing and resizing affect the texture of the leaf and usually leave a smell, faint but unnatural. Recasing leaves a stiff back and often scraped top edges into the bargain. New endpapers, though they fit to a millimetre, somehow never lie quite snug. And even if these obvious evidences are lacking, there is a special feel, indefinable but to the seasoned or sensitive hand (if on its guard) unmistakable, about a book which has once been divorced from its covers.

Should the critic be satisfied, or even strongly suspicious, of this, the book can expect little mercy, the benefit of no doubt. For once it is shown to have been out of its covers, what but that absent indelible note can testify that it was put back in the same covers? Leaves may have been substituted or washed, bookplates may have been switched, title-pages tampered with, endpapers renewed—anything is possible. And since not all doctoring is honest in intention, the critic will reasonably presume the worst. Nor, unless the book is of some considerable value even in sophisticated condition, is it worth his while to make that doubly meticulous examination which might find it innocent on some, if not all, of the

---

[1] Douglas Cockerell provided a regular label, on which the exact particulars could be entered, if the owner so desired.

possible counts. A restored copy of Juliana Berners's *Treatise of Hawking and Heraldry* (St Alban's, 1486), of Howard's *Songes and Sonettes* (1557), even of *Songs of Innocence and Experience* (1789–94) or of the Bristol *Lyrical Ballads* (1798) would be scrutinised leaf by leaf, its faults set out alongside its merits; and the result would still be something of consequence. But a doctored *Eothen* (1844), *Vanity Fair* (1848) or *The Portrait of a Lady* (3 vols., 1881) is practically worthless. It is the belated recognition of this state of affairs, in an era of collecting strongly prejudiced in favour of original condition, which has led many contemporary collectors and most prudent booksellers to let well alone unless a book is hopelessly dilapidated: to prefer an untouched copy in fair or even moderate condition to another which owes either its soundness or its gloss to the restorer's art.

I propose to conclude this examination of a highly controversial subject with an appeal—not my first,[1] and not with any very lively anticipation of being listened to—an appeal to reason. There is no aspect of collecting technique on which the connoisseurs are so variously opinioned, so vocal and so intolerant of heterodox opinions: no area in which dictated criteria have been more ruthlessly applied, in which tastes have more often become fetiches, in which reason has more repeatedly been stifled by rules. If it is obligatory, as in my view it is, that the functional relationship between original boards and original leather should be more generally appreciated, it is certainly time also to rid ourselves of the tyranny of the uncut edge. To books in original boards, wrappers or cloth, untrimmed edges are natural and proper, and in such copies they are rightly insisted upon. But an eighteenth- or early nineteenth-century book with uncut edges in a modern levant binding is an unnatural object, and it is a false tradition which has elevated it to preference over another copy in a contemporary (even if not actually a trade) binding, the edges of which will normally be, as they were meant to be, cut.

[1] Cf. John Carter, 'Original Condition, an appeal to reason' in *The Publisher's Weekly*, 15 November 1930.

Even the tyranny of original cloth becomes unbearable on occasions, for it is sometimes applied without that sense of proportion which alone prevents book-collecting from becoming the foppish preciosity for which its critics sometimes mistake it. The strong preference for original cloth and, among verse and *belles lettres* of the past hundred years, for its publisher's boards or wrappers, is a sound and a rational development, never likely to be abrogated by future changes of taste. Yet there are a fair number of such books which are so rare in their original state that for the ordinary collector they might as well not exist. Is he to pine for the moon, like his neighbour who is hopelessly waiting for *Pamela* (4 vols., 1741–2) in boards? Or will he consider the notion that *Wuthering Heights* (3 vols., 1847) or FitzGerald's *Omar* (1859) in a pleasing contemporary binding is no more contemptible than a first issue of *Tales of My Landlord*, first series (4 vols., Edinburgh, 1816) or Landor's *Simonidea* (Bath, 1806) in similar condition?

Standards are not betrayed by being made subject in their application to the laws of relativity, and Draconic legislation has been known to defeat its own ends. We may surely be realistic in the face of nineteenth-century rarities as well as fifteenth-century. Moreover, those of us who like to handle our books live face to face with the problem of combining use and enjoyment with the preservation of fragility. Anyone whose collection includes books in boards, wrappers or cloth knows the perils which beset him. He takes great risks if he keeps them on a shelf in the ordinary way, for either dryness or damp has a devastating effect; boards crack, wrappers curl up, flimsy cloth cockles and fades; while a single piece of careless handling may be fatal to these delicate perfections. What is he to do? More and more he is driven to the use of boxes, slip-cases and the like, which are tiresome to deal with, expensive to make and ruinous to the appearance of his library. If it is a time-honoured charge that collectors never read their books, it must be admitted that it costs a man five pounds every time he reads his first edition of *Lamia* (1820) in boards: and we are not all millionaires. Moreover this tendency has one particularly vicious result—sometimes a collector will prefer a book for which he really cares less because its condition is more enticing; and book-collecting will have come to a pretty pass when sound endpapers are of more account than good writing.

I must not be thought to suggest that collectors should be anything but fastidious in their choice of copies, persistent in their pursuit of better ones and faithful to their preferences, whether for the original or the appropriate in condition. But some of them might be happier men and not less admired performers if they were less hidebound by bibliophilic conventions and more realistic, even within their own orbit of taste, in their appreciation of what is attainable and what is not. Mr Sadleir, whose worst enemy would not accuse him of being easy-going in this respect, once wrote[1] of a rare Victorian novel in terms which have a more than particular application. 'It can hardly be subject [he said] to the usual considerations of condition. A fine copy (if one exists) will of course out-value those less perfect, but collectors should realise that they neglect even a bad copy at their peril. They may never see another.'

[1] *Trollope, a Bibliography*, p. 260.

INDEX

BY THE SAME AUTHOR

Binding Variants in English Publishing, 1820–1900
Bibliographia Series, No. 6. 1932.

More Binding Variants
Aspects of Book-Collecting Series. 1938.

Publisher's Cloth, an outline history. 1935

New Paths in Book-Collecting
Essays by various hands, edited by John Carter. 1934.

Sir Thomas Browne's *Urne Buriall and The Garden of Cyrus*
Edited with an apparatus criticus by John Carter. 1932.

WITH GRAHAM POLLARD
An Enquiry into the Nature of Certain Nineteenth Century Pamphlets. 1934
The Firm of Charles Ottley, Landon & Co. Footnote to an enquiry. 1948.

WITH MICHAEL SADLEIR
Victorian Fiction. 1947.

WITH JOHN SPARROW
A. E. Housman, an annotated check-list. 1940.

WITH BROOKE CRUTCHLEY
Aldis. *The Printed Book,* revised edition. 1941.